The Intelligent

Small Investor

Ordinary People

Become Millionaires

David S. J. Meng

To my wife and children.
To my parents, who persevered through poverty and hunger to raise three kids and send them to college. In memory of my father, whose late hobby was planting beautiful flowers and trees before he passed away on December 15, 2018.

Our Humble Net Worth

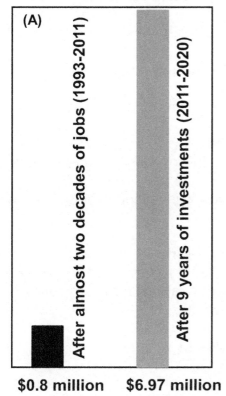

(A)

After almost two decades of jobs (1993-2011)

After 9 years of investments (2011-2020)

$0.8 million   **$6.97 million**

Annual Growth Rate

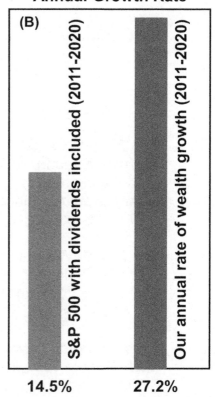

(B)

S&P 500 with dividends included (2011-2020)

Our annual rate of wealth growth (2011-2020)

14.5%   **27.2%**

(A) My wife and I are ordinary employees. Working hard at our jobs from 1993-2011 produced $0.8 million for our net worth. My daughter's sickness in 2010 gave me a wake-up call to invest for financial security, and we started investing in 2011. By the end of 2020, our net worth reached $6.97 million.

(B) Our annual wealth growth rate averaged 27.2%, exceeding 14.5% of S&P 500 (2011-2020). This book shows how small investors and ordinary people can use novel "Money Tree" methods to make millions and reach financial freedom.

Table of Contents

Introduction   7

1.   Real-Life Examples of Planting Money Trees   16

2.   Conventional Wisdom Kills Financial Freedom   24

3.   The Early Bird Gets the Worm   32
      Myth: I am young, so, if I delay investing by a few years,
      it's not a big deal.
      Money Tree: An ounce of early investing is better than a
      pound of late investing.

4.   The Eighth Wonder of the World   42
      Myth: A 2% difference in rate of return is not a big deal.
      Money Tree: Increasing your rate of return by just 2%
      can double or triple your wealth.

5.   Career Choice toward Wealth   48
      Myth: Pursue your passion.
      Money Tree: Bridge your passion with a lucrative field,
      and combine the two. Combination is creation.

6.   The Joy of Home Ownership   62
      Myth: You should rent and not buy a house unless you
      will stay in the house for at least 5 years.
      Money Tree: Analyze case by case. Even 2-3 years of
      living in the house often yields substantial profits.

7.   A Mortgage-Free Life Costs You Millions   74
      Myth: Prepay and pay off your mortgage, then live
      mortgage-free.
      Money Tree: Use your house as the "mother" tree to
      breed more money trees.

8.   Give Me a Lever and I Can Move the Earth   87

Myth: Leverage is risky.
Money Tree: Grow wealth by maintaining leverage.

9. **Positive Carry** 96
Myth: Live a debt-free and interest-free life.
Money Tree: Positive carry + compounding is a simple method to plant money trees and make millions.

10. **My Crystal Ball Is in the Repair Shop** 105
Myth: Predict and time the market to get rich.
Money Tree: Keep investing intelligently and persistently for a decade, and you will reach financial freedom.

11. **Do You Have Cash Flow or Alligators?** 117
Myth: They both have $3 million, so they are the same.
Money Tree: Build up cash flow. Avoid alligators.

12. **Retire in Your 40s?** 125
Myth: Can ordinary working-class people achieve financial freedom and retire in their 40s? No way!
Money Tree: Can ordinary people achieve early retirement and financial freedom? Yes we can!

13. **It's Not the Strongest, Nor the Fastest, But the Most Persistent, Who Will Succeed** 134
Myth: Whether or not you can achieve financial freedom depends on your salary level.
Money Tree: A decade of persistence leads to life-long financial independence.

14. **The Return Is the King** 141
Myth: Cash is king.
Money Tree: The rate of return is king.

15. **These Mutual Funds All Look Similar** 154
Myth: Just pick a few mutual funds and they are all pretty much the same.

Money Tree: Simple choice, life-changing difference.

16. **It's Just 1%. What's the Big Deal?** 165
Myth: A 1% mutual fund fee is no big deal.
Money Tree: A 1% mutual fund fee can cost you millions of dollars.

17. **Work Harder and Lose Money?** 174
Myth: I can pick stocks to invest and beat the market.
Money Tree: Spend less time and make millions more.

18. **This Sounds Too Easy to Be True** 185
Myth: Start a business and work really hard to get rich.
Money Tree: Intelligent small investors spend less time and outperform most startups and big companies.

19. **Another 10X to Your Wealth** 192
Myth: By age 50, you should have already made the bulk of your money.
Money Tree: Grow wealth by another 10x after age 50.

20. **Make More Money Passively in Your Retirement than Working Hard at a Job** 200
Myth: After you retire, move money to CDs, bonds and mutual funds, and rebalance annually.
Money Tree: Two years of living expenses in cash, everything else in S&P 500.

21. **The Eagle's Two Wings: Courage and Caution** 216
Myth: Fearless.
Money Tree: Balance.

22. **No Pain, Much Gain** 226
Myth: No pain, no gain.
Money Tree: No pain, much gain. Staying calm, joyful and thankful enhances wealth growth.

Introduction

My wife and I are self-made millionaires, having grown our net worth from humble beginnings to nearly $7 million in 2020.

In 2010, my daughter was hospitalized for three weeks with a life-threatening infection after a serious misdiagnosis. It was my wake-up call that my family needed financial security to weather unforeseen circumstances. There in the hospital, I made up my mind to learn to invest.

My experience as a small investor from 2011-2019 is summarized in my first book, *$5 Million in 8 Years: Real Estate Investing on the Side*. Readers have praised it on Amazon:[2]

"Very inspiring life-changing book."

"I wish I had read this book years ago."

"I am a well-established real estate investor. I have read many real estate books. This book is among the best."

"I have read so many books, ... This book is different. ... I highly recommend this book to new and seasoned investor."

"This has been by far the best book that I have read."

This feedback, and the people whom I have been able to help, have inspired me to write this second book.

The Purpose of This Book. This book will empower and enrich ordinary people, stop myths and conventional "wisdom" from robbing people millions of dollars, and show "money tree" methods for people to achieve financial freedom.

This book is for ordinary people, including high school and college students, young professionals, renters, homeowners, middle-aged employees, real estate investors, mutual fund investors, 401k investors, IRA and Roth IRA investors, low income and high income earners, and retirees.

Benjamin Franklin said: "An investment in knowledge pays the best interest."

If you could invest $20 in a book that would help you make millions, would you do it? If you could invest a few hours in reading a book that would help you reach your dream of financial freedom, retire early, and enjoy financial security and quality of life with your loved ones, would you do it?

If you think that making millions is impossible and financial freedom is too big a dream for you, remember what Robert Frost said: "Freedom lies in being bold."[1]

You would be bold to learn to make millions by growing money trees, and your financial freedom lies in your being bold.

When my children were little, I read them the Magic Tree House series, which taught us that "Reading is the magic key to take you where you want to be." I wrote this book to serve as the "magic key" to take you to the land of financial freedom.

Mr. Warren Buffett started investing in stocks at a young age. However, for years, he struggled to find the way. Then, one day, he came across the book, *The Intelligent Investor*, by Mr. Benjamin Graham. Reading that book changed Buffett's life; it was like "seeing the light".[3]

The Intelligent Investor benefited Buffett, and it's my hope that *The Intelligent Small Investor: Ordinary People Become Millionaires* will benefit you.

As Buffett's partner, Mr. Charlie Munger, put it: "Ben Graham was a truly formidable mind. And he also had a clarity in writing. And we've talked over and over again about the power of a few simple ideas thoroughly assimilated."[4]

The purpose of this book is to provide ordinary people the power of a few simple ideas thoroughly assimilated.

I am a small potato compared to billionaires. However, books about billionaires involve strategies that are not readily applicable to ordinary people. In contrast, the simple ideas in this book are executable and reproducible by ordinary people.

The Harm of Financial Myths and Conventional "Wisdom". I am sad to see financial myths and conventional "wisdom" killing the financial freedom of people.

Conventional wisdom is often accepted without question; while some parts are good, others may be wrong and harmful. It takes courage to question conventional wisdom. For example, it was once conventional wisdom that the earth was flat, and that the earth was the center of the universe.

Financial myths and false conventional wisdom make people lose millions of dollars. Here is a myth for the young professionals: "I'm so young. I can wait. If I delay investing by a few years, what's the big deal?" Well, as shown in an example in Chapter 3, such a delay can cost you $4 million.

For high school and college students, selecting a major and a career is one of their most important decisions. They are often told: "Pursue your passion!" This book presents a unique "combination is creation" approach that can enable you to: (1) earn millions more in your career, (2) pursue your passion, and (3) make full use of your talents to contribute to the society, as shown in the examples in Chapter 5.

Here is another myth: "Mutual funds are quite similar. Just pick a few funds to put your money in." This myth, as shown in Chapter 15, can cost an ordinary person $3.8 million. Chapter 15 solves the mystery of why an ordinary employee cannot accumulate millions in his or her 401k account.

In Chapter 15, the simple "money-tree method" of this book can help the ordinary employee accumulate $4.5 million.

Here is another myth: "A 1% fee charged by mutual funds is not a big deal. 1% is small and negligible." Using average mutual funds with average fees can make you lose $3.49 million in profits that otherwise would be yours to enjoy, as illustrated in one of the examples in Chapter 16.

Many believe: "Small investors and everyday people cannot beat the gurus." Chapter 18 lays out a simple strategy for the ordinary person to outperform the big professionals, obtain higher returns, and achieve financial freedom.

I have heard this piece of conventional wisdom quite frequently: "Prepay your mortgage and pay it off early. It saves you interest money." As shown in an example in Chapter 7, this can cost an ordinary person more than $6 million.

This book demonstrates the intelligent use of mortgages to maintain leverage and plant money trees, whether to buy rental properties or simply to invest passively in an index fund (such as the S&P 500). As shown in the examples of Chapter 7, this money-tree method can produce approximately $6 million to $80 million for an ordinary family.

The following myth has also become popular: "Live a debt-free life! Debt-free is the new rich!"

This myth can cost millions of dollars and destroy opportunities for people to achieve financial freedom. A knife can be used to harm people; does this mean that we should live a "knife-free life"? A knife can also be used to prepare food to feed people. This book shows the use of good debt to grow millions of dollars of extra wealth for you and your loved ones.

In addition, some myths say that you have to work hard to do research on stocks and trade often, in order to get rich. This book debunks these myths, consistent with what Mr. Warrant Buffett said: "There seems to be some perverse human characteristic that likes to make easy things difficult."[5] This book shows money tree methods to make millions that are easy, simple, and even "do-nothing." For example, Chapter 17 describes a motto: LWMW (less work, more wealth).

Financial Freedom. If you think that the numbers of $3 million or $6 million are too big for you, I hope the example of me, an ordinary person from humble beginnings, can help give you courage. As the French poet Charles Peguy said:

"Freedom is a system based on courage."[6]

Your courage and ability to think big will help lead you to the land of financial freedom. So, what is financial freedom?

Financial freedom is a state of life that is free from worrying about money, free from being mastered by jobs and bosses, free to enjoy more choices, and free to live life on your terms and to the fullest.

Financial freedom removes the anxiety of living paycheck to paycheck, the fear of being laid off by the company, and the worries of putting a roof over one's family and putting food on the table.

Financial freedom leads to time freedom. I remember seeing a definition of work as: "Every morning, millions of parents are taken away from their homes by a horrible thing called work." Financial freedom means that you have time to spend with your loved ones, have time to sleep in, have time to visit Europe or Asia whenever you like, and do not have to sit in traffic jams, go to boring meetings and be stuck at your work.

Financial freedom leads to life freedom. You don't have to say "yes" to a nasty boss. You don't have to work with jerks. Money does not control your life. You are the master of money. You have the freedom to live your life on your own terms.

Financial freedom enables you to pursue your life's passions, without worrying about money. You have the money and the time to pursue your hobbies and other dreams. Financial freedom provides you with the capability to fully experience the goodness of life.

Financial freedom enables you to help others, give back, make an impact, and thereby be rewarded with a satisfying life.

How do we achieve financial freedom? This book shows how to grow money trees so that your money will grow day and night, year after year. You will be making money while vacationing in Europe, on a cruise ship, and in your sleep.

Think Independently and Outside of the Box. The money tree methods of this book are unorthodox, innovative, and simple. They debunk popular financial myths and overturn harmful conventional "wisdom".

Only a small percentage of people become self-made millionaires. Assume that out of 10,000 adults, only 10 are self-made millionaires. If you want to become one of them, you will need to be among the minority group of 10. Therefore, you cannot go with the crowd of 9,990, even if being in the big crowd makes you feel more comfortable, with a false sense of safety. That means at times you have to go against the crowd, question popular "wisdom", and resist herd thinking.

As Mark Twain said: "Whenever you find yourself on the side of the majority, it is time to pause and reflect."[7]

By thinking independently and outside of the box, you will be rewarded with millions of dollars to provide yourself and your loved ones with financial security and freedom.

This Book Helps You Break Away from Myths and So-Called "Conventional Wisdom." Many myths and misunderstandings about money and investing have blinded people's financial eyes, bound their hands, limited their minds, and cost them millions of dollars that otherwise could have been used by them and their loved ones to enjoy life.

Granted, many people feel safer inside the box and inside the crowd, and are fearful of going against popular conventional wisdom. However, as Robert H. Schuller said:

"If you listen to your fears, you will die never knowing what a great person you might have been."[8]

This book helps you demolish these myths and fears in your thought process. This book debunks conventional "wisdom" that has hindered numerous people, robbed them of their financial freedom, and degraded their quality of life.

This book shows you how to plant "money trees." Then,

money will grow on trees for you. You will achieve financial security for yourself and your loved ones, have time to pursue your passions, and have the ability to give and help others.

This book shows think-outside-of-the-box, practical, executable, and reproducible methods. It shows lucrative, yet simple strategies to make millions. This book provides courage and safeguards to help you get started and take action.

The Structure of This Book. This book first presents real-life deals of my wife and I, showing what ordinary people can become through the applications of this book. This is followed by presenting the urgent need to learn to invest. This book then shows novel money-tree methods for career choices for high school and college students, and lucrative and simple investing methods for young professionals and homeowners. This is followed by the intelligent use of leverage, mutual fund selections, real estate, as well as wealth creation for middle-aged employees, 50-year olds, and retirees. Besides building up the physical strength and technical skills, this book ends with building up the inner emotional strength for the investor.

The great American writer and lecturer Dale Carnegie said: "Inaction breeds doubt and fear. Action breeds confidence and courage. If you want to conquer fear, do not sit at home and think about it. Go out and get busy."[9]

This book will help you pull the trigger and take action. Let's get busy and start your journey toward financial freedom!

Chapter 1. Real-Life Examples of Planting Money Trees

1. A Townhouse Rental Property as a Money Tree

My wife and I invest in both real estate and the stock market. For our rental properties, I use a team to help me, so that I need to spend only a few hours per week. Here is an example about a townhouse that we bought in 2011. It has three stories with about 2,000 square feet, with beautiful wall paintings and elegant decorations throughout the house, which my wife fell in love with. The house has a huge open backyard that our real estate agent called "the million-dollar view". The price was $272,000. We paid a 20% down payment of $54,400, and obtained a 30-year fixed mortgage from a bank. We paid a bit more than $10,000 for closing costs and to a handyman to get the house ready for rent. So, the total amount of money that we threw into this house was about $65,000.

The house is located in an excellent school district. My agent helped rent it to a family at a rent of $1,995/month.

Think of this house as a money tree. We harvest three types of "fruits" from this tree.

First, cash flow. The net positive cash flow, after deducting all expenses including mortgage and repairs, is about $300/month. This equals $3,600 of cash flow annually.

Second, principal reduction. The mortgage payment includes interest, principal, insurance, and property tax. The principal is basically paid into our own pocket, because it reduces the loan that we owe the bank. The principal amount increases with time, and the interest amount decreases over time, as we owe less and less money to the bank. In December 2020, the principal amount is about $400/month. This equals to a principal reduction of $4,800 annually.

Third, house value appreciation. According to www.zillow.com, in December 2020, the estimated price for this house is $382,582. Hence, it has appreciated by more than $100,000 since 2011. By December 2020, we still owe the bank about $167,000. Therefore, we have more than $200,000 of equity in this house.

Therefore, once you plant a money tree, you harvest these fruits. My wife and I plan to hold this money tree for the long term. We have grown our investment portfolio to nearly twenty money trees including rentals and mutual funds.

2. A Commercial Property Using Other People's Money

In 2017, my wife and I bought a commercial property. I found a friend to be my partner at a 50% share each. The price was $1.9 million. My part of the down payment was about

$200,000, which I obtained from lender A. The rest was a mortgage from lender B. Therefore, my wife and I did not have our own money in this rental property.

Here are the three types of fruits from this money tree.

First, cash flow. The net positive cash flow (after deducting all expenses such as mortgages, insurance, etc.) was $21,000/year for the share of my wife and I.

Second, principal reduction. At the end of 2020, the mortgage statement showed the principal payment to be $3,377.75. This number increases over time as we owe less and less money to the lender. For a simple estimate, assume that the principal part was approximately the same as being $3,377.75 for the past year. $3,377.75 x 12 months = $40,533. My wife and I own 50% of this property. Hence, our part of principal reduction was about $20,000.

Third, appreciation. We have a long-term tenant with a lease where the rent increases by 3% per year. The commercial property value is usually tied with the rental income. Hence, we assume that the property value increases by 3% annually. It has been three years. Hence, the current value = $1.9 million x 1.03 x 1.03 x 1.03 = $2.08 million. Therefore, this property appreciated by about $180,000 in three years. The appreciation in the last year for our 50% share was about $30,000.

The annual fruits from this money tree: $21,000 (cash flow) + $20,000 (principal reduction) + $30,000 (appreciation) = $71,000.

My wife and I are ordinary small investors, and these may be small money trees. But they will grow in the coming years. As Warren Buffett said: "Someone is sitting in the shade today because someone planted a tree a long time ago."[1]

You can also plant money trees so that you and your loved ones will be sitting in the shade and enjoying the fruits.

3. Investing in the S&P 500 Using Other People's Money

In addition to real estate, my wife and I also invest in mutual funds, namely, the S&P 500.

By 2020, we had significant equity in our real estate properties. We had two options: (1) Let the equity sit in the properties doing nothing, and (2) borrow money from the lenders using the equity to plant a money tree.

In spring 2020, I used a commercial line of credit with a local bank to borrow money to invest in the S&P 500. In the summer, I used a home equity line of credit. Then in the fall, we did a cash-out refinance on two of our townhouses and poured the cash into the S&P 500. We used a total of three lenders in 2020 to borrow money to invest in the S&P 500.

From March through October 2020, we invested a total of $1,075,000 into the S&P 500. Our S&P 500 balance as of 12/31/2020: $1,374,723. The net growth in 2020: $299,723.

The $1,075,000 was borrowed from three lenders. We need to pay interest to the lenders. The total interest payment in 2020 for these loans was about $16,500.

The money that this tree produced in 2020: Approximately $283,000.

This is the amount of net positive money grown by this tree in 2020 alone. It will grow more money in the future as we plan to hold it for longer than a decade.

In a number of years, this S&P 500 investment will double. At that point, we could choose to repay the lenders the borrowed money, and keep the $1 million profit. This was obtained by using other people's money, and spending only a few hours of my time. The rate of return (net profit/invested capital out of our pocket = profit/0) could be considered infinite. This would be like growing $1 million of profit out of thin air.

Making profits using other people's money and spending little of my time. It was like growing money out of thin air.

How should we control the risk? The S&P 500 goes up and down. Its rate of return on average from 1965-2020 is 10% per year. We plan to hold this investment for the long term.

Some people think that investments are risky. However, not investing is even more risky, due to not achieving financial security for the family. Indeed, as Mellody Hobson said:

"The biggest risk of all is not taking one."[2]

To minimize the risks, I use two weapons: (1) dollar cost averaging, (2) holding for the long term. My wife and I plan to do cash-out refinances every year or every couple of years, whenever some of our properties have accumulated sufficient equity. Then we plan to invest the cash into the S&P 500.

If the S&P 500 crashes in 2021, we plan to put more money into it to buy low. If it crashes in 2022, we plan to put more money into it to buy low, and so on. While other investors do monthly dollar cost averaging, ours could be called annual dollar cost averaging. We plan to hold this money tree for the long term to grow a bigger tree and harvest more money.

4. Other Index Funds, Mutual Funds and Exchange-Traded Funds (ETFs)

The above example uses the S&P 500. However, the methods of this book are not limited to the S&P 500. There are other types of index funds, mutual funds, hedge funds, and ETFs that an investor can choose. I would keep in mind the following checklist for selecting a good fund.

21

(1) I would make sure that the fund fees are super low, and the rate of return is similar to, or better than, the S&P 500 index. If the other fund choice is not better than the S&P 500, then I would just stick with the S&P 500.

(2) It is good to examine the long-term track record for several decades when selecting a fund. This will help avoid chasing the hot fund that achieves a great return this year, but would become mediocre in subsequent years.

(3) Furthermore, be aware that some funds would do well for a decade because it has been run by an exceptional fund manager. Then the star manager retires or leaves, and the star fund becomes mediocre. For this reason, I use the S&P 500 because it does not depend on a star manager.

(4) There are other index funds and ETFs with low fees. You may select one of them. Just make sure that the fund's long-term rate of return is as good as, if not better than, the S&P 500. Also make sure that the fund includes a sufficient number of diversified companies so that it is not too volatile. For example, the S&P 500 includes 500 large companies.

(5) Beware of mutual funds that focus on a certain section that performs exceptionally well for a certain period of time. For example, in the 1990s, mutual funds that focused on technology made high returns. However, they crashed and dropped much more than the S&P 500 in 2001 and 2002.

(6) It is also important that the fund is easy to invest in, and is readily available in 401k accounts if you are selecting it for your 401k account.

Once you have selected your favorite fund or a few funds, just substitute all mentions of "the S&P 500" in this book with your selected fund or funds. The same methods described in this book will still apply, and similar investment results will still be obtained, if your selected funds satisfy the aforementioned checklist.

As Charlie Munger wisely advises:

"No wise pilot, no matter how great his talent and experience, fails to use his checklist."[3]

Important Point. Prior to 2010, as an ordinary employee, I could not have imagined doing the investments such as those described in this chapter, moving million-dollar capitals, and making these profits. My humble experience shows that if one is willing to learn and take action to invest, there is so much that one can achieve in a decade. If I can help a few people do this, then this book has fulfilled its mission.

Remember: "Fortune sides with him or her who dares."

My wife and I are ordinary working-class people from humble beginnings. This book shows how ordinary people can plant money trees and harvest their financial freedom.

Chapter 2. Conventional Wisdom Kills Financial Freedom

1. The Importance of Investing and Financial Freedom

I hope that the real-life examples of my wife and I in Chapter 1 bring you inspiration. There is an urgent need for us to learn to invest for the financial security of our families.

In the several months from April to October 2020, I have personally known eight people, some of them dear friends, who were laid off due to the Covid-19 pandemic. One close friend lost his job when his entire department was closed. He has three children to support and the family just moved into a bigger house a year ago. His first child is in college, and his second will start college soon, with tuitions to be paid.

I know several families in which the husband went to China because he found a job there, and the wife and kids are staying in the United States. They see each other for only a few weeks per year. They are hard-working people and are making a sacrifice for a better future for the children. The employment in China (or for that matter, in any other foreign country, or in another city away from home) earns an income for the family, but they pay a dear price for it. They are providing for the family, but miss the spousal time together and watching the kids growing up, which is priceless and irreversible.

Therefore, we need to learn to invest to achieve financial freedom, so that we can avoid being forced to choose between job income and family staying together.

This book provides these and other similar families with a better option. For example, using the methods described in Chapter 13, the family can stay together, earn millions of dollars, and achieve financial freedom.

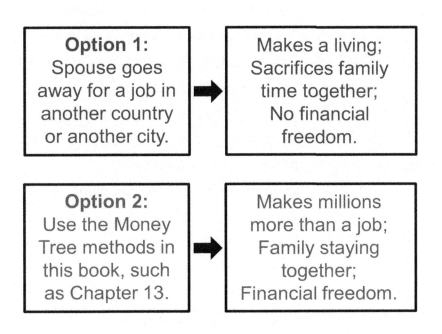

You likely also have friends or classmates who were laid off. The number of unemployed workers from April to June 2020 shot up to historically high unemployment rates, devastating the finances of numerous families. Experts predict a painful and long process, likely taking years, to replace the jobs lost.

Layoffs occur quite frequently. During the 2008-2009 great recession, the unemployment rate was doubled from about 5% to 10%. More than 15 million people in the United States were unemployed near the end of 2009.[1]

Even during economically good times, people are laid off simply because jobs are outsourced to less expensive countries, company restructuring to cut costs, or automation. Job security is becoming more and more a thing of the past.

Even social security is not "secure" anymore. It is estimated that by 2034, the program will have to reduce the payout to just 77% of the scheduled payments.[2] In addition, the 77% will likely be further reduced in subsequent years.

We look forward to the day of retirement when we are finally relieved of job-related stresses and anxieties, traffic jams, and company politics. People happily say:

"I'm retired – goodbye tension, hello pension!"

Well, with baby-boomers retiring en masse, the number of seniors withdrawing money from pensions is increasing dramatically. On the other hand, fewer young people are joining the pension plans. Like social security, the pension may not be there anymore when you need it in the future.

Therefore, now more than ever, we need to take our financial future into our own hands. We need to learn the best investing methods to achieve financial freedom for ourselves and our loved ones. This is the purpose for my writing this book.

2. Schools Do Not Teach Investing and How to Reach Financial Freedom

Money is not everything. However, money is important in life. People lose their homes due to the lack of money. People cannot afford life-saving therapies and medicine due to the lack of money. Many people work long hours or even two or three jobs to support their family. Therefore, money is an important part of daily life.

Important Point. Knowing how to invest to reach financial freedom is one of the most important skills in life.

Unfortunately, while many of us spend 16+ years in schools to learn skills to work in engineering, science or medical fields, we spend virtually no time learning about critically-important investing skills to reach financial freedom.

No wonder people say, "Money talks ... but all mine ever says is goodbye."

In typical elementary through high schools, there is little teaching on money and investing. All through our college and graduate educations, my wife and I received not a single course on finance and investing. As a result, all my wife and I knew was to work hard, be frugal and save.

This situation lasted until 2010, when a serious sickness and prolonged hospitalization of my daughter gave me the wake-up call. I started to invest in 2011 in order to secure a financial foundation for my family. I studied hundreds of books on investing and put them to practice on my own.

This has made a big difference in our wealth growth. Working hard for 17 years brought our net worth in 2011 to $0.8 million. Investing for half that time brought our net worth to nearly $7 million in 2020. Investing grew our wealth many times more than working our day jobs.

This is attainable to you too as a "small investor". Indeed, the purpose of this book is to inspire more and more people to learn investing and realize their dream of financial freedom.

The wealth of my wife and I is tiny compared to billionaires. However, the investing methods of billionaires, involving large sums of movements and specialized strategies, are not applicable to the ordinary person. In contrast, the practical and highly profitable methods that I describe in this book are more suitable and applicable to, and reproducible by, the ordinary people.

3. Unorthodox, Think-outside-of-the-Box "Money Tree" Methods Make Millions

People say: "Money doesn't grow on trees."

However, wouldn't it be nice if money could grow on trees for you?

This book teaches ordinary people how to plant money trees so that your money will grow on trees.

My father passed away on December 15, 2018. In his career, he built houses for other people, working days and evenings and weekends. His skill and craftsmanship was recognized as the best for miles in the village where I grew up. My family struggled in the 1960s and 1970s, lacking food, feeling hungry most of the time, lacking warm clothes in bitter-cold winter without heating, and walking around bare foot most of the year except in winter. My parents' hard work supported the family through poverty and famine, and helped send all three kids to colleges.

Later, when the financial situation started to improve in the 1990s, my parents developed a hobby for gardening. My father planted beautiful flowers and trees, both in ground and in pots. He then multiplied the plants into hundreds, by breeding baby plants from the mother plants.

This book shows how to breed and multiple your money trees. For example, Chapter 8 shows how to use the equity in the house as the mother tree to breed money trees that can grow an extra $10 million for an ordinary family, compared to that without using the money tree method.

In addition, Chapters 12 and 13 show that, by using the money tree methods, ordinary people with ordinary income can retire comfortably in their 40s.

It is common belief that we should have made the bulk of our wealth by the time we reach the age of 50. However, Chapter 19 demonstrates that we can multiple our wealth by 10x after age 50. We can increase our wealth by at least an order of magnitude after age 50, using the money tree methods, without having to work hard.

Chapter 20 illustrates that the money tree methods can grow far more money, passively, in our retirement, than working hard at a job. In an example, the money tree method can grow at least $6 million more wealth for you, without needing your effort, while you enjoy your retirement.

You may ask: "Wow, it's great that the money tree methods can produce millions of dollars of wealth for me. But does it involve extra hard work? My life is already busy, and I do not want to give up my hobbies and free time."

A big merit of the money tree methods, described in this book, is the focus on simplicity and "do-nothing".

In investing, "money is like soap; the more you handle it, the less you will have."[3]

Compared to many of the conventional wisdom and myths, the innovative and unconventional money tree methods will make millions more, while taking up much less of our time (for examples, see Chapters 17 and 18).

Important Points. The money tree methods are powerful wealth-building machines that are think-outside-of-the-box, unorthodox, highly lucrative, and simple.

The Structure of the Following Chapters. The subsequent chapters are structured with each chapter starting with a popular "Myth", along with a "Money Tree" counterpoint. In this way, each chapter debunks a popular myth or conventional wisdom that can cause substantial financial harm. The chapter then describes a corresponding innovative and think-outside-of-the-box money tree method that can grow millions of dollars of wealth in a simple and executable way for ordinary people.

Chapter 3. The Early Bird Catches the Worm

Myth: **I am young, so, if I delay investing by a few years, it's not a big deal.**

Money Tree: **An ounce of early investing is better than a pound of late investing.**

"Money is good; shop till you drop."

"Money is bad. As soon as you have some, get rid of it by spending it all."

"The only exercise I've had this month is running – out of money."

My wife and I have three kids. Our oldest daughter, Sweetie, graduated from college in 2017 at the age of 22 and started working for a big company. Sweetie is smart, funny, beautiful and kind. She can roll over the floor laughing at her own jokes. She is a dancer, and she and her husband Moutai are avid rock-climbers. She donated bone marrow to save an unknown patient. She and Moutai flew to South America to adopt a dog from a shelter, because no one wanted the dogs there. They give to their church and charities and help the poor. She has been volunteering to teach English to new immigrants.

As of writing this book in 2020, she is 25 years old and her salary is about $70,000. One day, at dinner, we started to talk about money.

I asked her: "Can you save $10,000 per year?"

She said with her typical shiny optimistic smile: "Yes, I think I can. I mean, wouldn't someone else whose salary is $60,000 or $50,000 also make a living?"

She is absolutely right. The next day, I did the following calculation.

1. Scenario 1: Delayed Gratification

In this illustration, assume that Sweetie chooses delayed gratification. Assume that starting from her new job at the age of 22, she saves $10,000 each year and invests it in an S&P 500 index fund. She does this for 10 years until she is 31 years old, when she would have invested a total of $100,000 into the S&P 500.

Then after age 31, for the purpose of illustration, she stops saving and investing.

After age 31, she travels the world, and buys beautiful bags, lovely shoes and fancy clothes.

33

2. Scenario 2: Instant Gratification

In this illustration, assume that Sweetie's college classmate, Susan, chooses instant gratification. From age 22 to 31, Susan lives paycheck to paycheck with no savings, and spends the money on luxury items and eating out frequently. As some people would say:

"I am so young. I have many decades left before I retire. I can start investing at age 35 or 40. Right now, I just want to enjoy life and not worry about investing."

Then at the age of 32, Susan finally comes across this book by David Meng, which serves as a wake-up call. She decides to start investing. At age 32, she saves $10,000 each year and invests it in the S&P 500. She does it for 10 years and then stops investing. In this way, she puts in the same amount of $100,000 of principal into S&P 500 as in Scenario 1.

They invest the same amount of capital: $100,000.

They use the same S&P 500 index fund.

Each invests the same $10,000 per year for 10 years.

The only difference: Sweetie starts 10 years earlier than Susan.

How much money will they each have by the time they retire, say, at the age of 70?

The S&P 500 has ups and downs and booms and busts. But on average, from 1965-2020, with dividend reinvested, the S&P 500 index has returned 10% annually.

3. Some Math

Let's look at some math. Do not be scared of math. In most of the investing deals that I have done, elementary school math is sufficient. Therefore, please be confident that you can deal with the simple math.

Math is important in investing. It helps the investor to focus on numbers and not emotion. It helps the investor to have a clear sight of the rate of return. It enables the investor to rise above the trees to see the forest, and to block out the noise of the tree leaves which are blown this way today and that way tomorrow.

Indeed, as Warren Buffett's mentor Benjamin Graham said: "Buy not on optimism, but on arithmetic."

For example, your emotion may feel that method A is better than B. However, the math clearly shows that B is significantly better than A. Therefore, math can guide you to choose the right investment and make intelligent choices.

Another example: Your emotion may say that making $5 million is impossible for the ordinary person. But the math shows that using the methods described in this book, making $5 million can be accomplished indeed. Hence, math can help give you strength, confidence and determination.

Here is a quick review on the related math for this chapter. $10,000 invested at a 10% annual return becomes, after one year: $10,000 x 1.10 = $11,000.

After two years, it becomes: $10,000 x 1.10 x 1.10 =

$12,100

After 5 years, it becomes: $10,000 x 1.10 x 1.10 x 1.10 x 1.10 x 1.10 = $16,105.

After 48 years, it becomes: $10,000 x 1.10**48 = $0.97 million.

Here, the symbol ** means power. For example, 3**2 = 9. And 3**3 = 27.

4. Scenario 1: How Much Money Will Sweetie Have When She Reaches Age 70?

Now let's look at Sweetie's investment.

At age 22, Sweetie invests $10,000. From 22 to 70 is 48 years. $10,000 x 1.10**48 = $0.97 million.

At age 23, Sweetie invests $10,000. From 23 to 70 is 47 years. $10,000 x 1.10**47 = $0.88 million.

At age 24, Sweetie invests $10,000. From 24 to 70 is 46 years. $10,000 x 1.10**46 = $0.80 million.

At age 25, Sweetie invests $10,000. From 25 to 70 is 45 years. $10,000 x 1.10**45 = $0.73 million.

At age 26, Sweetie invests $10,000. From 26 to 70 is 44 years. $10,000 x 1.10**44 = $0.66 million.

At age 27, Sweetie invests $10,000. From 27 to 70 is 43 years. $10,000 x 1.10**43 = $0.60 million.

At age 28, Sweetie invests $10,000. From 28 to 70 is 42 years. $10,000 x 1.10**42 = $0.55 million.

At age 29, Sweetie invests $10,000. From 29 to 70 is 41

years. $10,000 \times 1.10^{**}41 = \$0.50$ million.

At age 30, Sweetie invests $10,000. From 30 to 70 is 40 years. $10,000 \times 1.10^{**}40 = \$0.45$ million.

At age 31, Sweetie invests $10,000. From 31 to 70 is 39 years. $10,000 \times 1.10^{**}39 = \$0.41$ million.

Total = $0.97 + $0.88 + $0.80 + $0.73 + $0.66 + $0.60 + $0.55 + $0.50 + $0.45 + $0.41 = $6.55 million.

Sweetie will have $6.55 million at the age of 70.

Do not be surprised by the seemingly big number. Due to inflation, the $6.55 million will be worth less when Sweetie reaches age 70, in terms of purchasing power. As people say:

"When I was younger, $20 felt like $100. Now, $20 feels like $5."

5. Scenario 2: How Much Money Will Susan Have When She Reaches Age 70?

Susan starts investing 10 years later than Sweetie.

At age 32, Susan invests $10,000. From 32 to 70 is 38 years. $10,000 \times 1.10^{**}38 = \$0.37$ million.

At age 33, Susan invests $10,000. From 33 to 70 is 37 years. $10,000 \times 1.10^{**}37 = \$0.34$ million.

At age 34, Susan invests $10,000. From 34 to 70 is 36 years. $10,000 \times 1.10^{**}36 = \$0.31$ million.

At age 35, Susan invests $10,000. From 35 to 70 is 35 years. $10,000 \times 1.10^{**}35 = \$0.28$ million.

At age 36, Susan invests $10,000. From 36 to 70 is 34 years. $10,000 x 1.10**34 = $0.26 million.

At age 37, Susan invests $10,000. From 37 to 70 is 33 years. $10,000 x 1.10**33 = $0.23 million.

At age 38, Susan invests $10,000. From 38 to 70 is 32 years. $10,000 x 1.10**32 = $0.21 million.

At age 39, Susan invests $10,000. From 39 to 70 is 31 years. $10,000 x 1.10**31 = $0.19 million.

At age 40, Susan invests $10,000. From 40 to 70 is 30 years. $10,000 x 1.10**30 = $0.17 million.

At age 41, Susan invests $10,000. From 41 to 70 is 29 years. $10,000 x 1.10**29 = $0.16 million.

Total = $0.37 + $0.34 + $0.31 + $0.28 + $0.26 + $0.23 + $0.21 + $0.19 + $0.17 + $0.16 = 2.52 million.

Susan will have $2.52 million at the age of 70.

Their difference: $6.55 - $2.52 = $4.03 million.

The delay in investing proves to be costly; the price tag in this example is $4.03 million.

And this assumes that Susan starts investing at age 32. Imagine that if she starts even later, say, at age 35 or 40, then her money at age 70 would be even less.

6. Money Tree: Grow Millions More by Investing Early

Important Point. By starting early in investing, you can have millions of extra dollars for yourself and your loved ones. I cannot overemphasize the importance of investing early. It means extra multimillions for an ordinary person. Indeed, an ounce of investing early is better than a pound of investing late.

I have made the calculation simple in order to illustrate the point, while not losing the reader. It assumes a single investment in one year. Usually you would invest every month. There are equations and Excel files to do more sophisticated calculations. I demonstrate it in this simple way because it is more straightforward, and you can see not only the end result, but also the middle process.

This will help you establish a vivid concept. This will also enable you to do your own estimates. Maybe John will invest $5,000 per year. Maybe Jack will invest $20,000 per year. Maybe you will start investing at age 25 or 28 or 33. Maybe you want to invest for 15 years and then stop, instead of 10 years. You can use the aforementioned way to do a simple estimate based on your own situation.

Many young people have student loans, and it is often not possible to start investing as early as 22 years of age. That is understandable. Maybe you can start investing at age 25. Maybe you can start at 27. In any case, it is highly beneficial to start investing as soon as possible, without delay.

Maybe you need to spend the first several years to pay off your student loans. Maybe you study for your PhD degree and start working when you are 29 years old. Maybe you are a medical doctor or a dentist, and do not earn a significant salary until after age 30. Whatever your situation, it will benefit you substantially and reward you with millions of dollars in extra wealth, if you start investing as soon as possible.

The math in this chapter illustrates the substantial benefits to minimize the living expenses in the early years with a delayed gratification, to save as much as possible, and to start investing as early as possible.

This doesn't mean that you will never spend money on luxury items and indulge yourself; only that you delay doing this by a number of years. Once a substantial amount is saved and invested (in this chapter's example, $100,000 over 10 years), you can then start to spend more freely. Importantly, because this method yields millions of dollars of extra wealth for you, you will actually have much more money to spend for yourself and for your loved ones.

Indeed, as Dave Ramsey said: "If you will make the sacrifices now that most people aren't willing to make, later on you will be able to live as those folks will never be able to live."[1]

Important Point. This chapter debunks the myth that delaying the investment by a few years, especially when you are young and in your 20s and early 30s, is not a big deal. This chapter establishes the money tree way: An ounce invested early is better than a pound invested late. By investing early, you can make millions of dollars in extra wealth. In addition, you can reach your dream of financial freedom, and quit your job and retire early if you so desire.

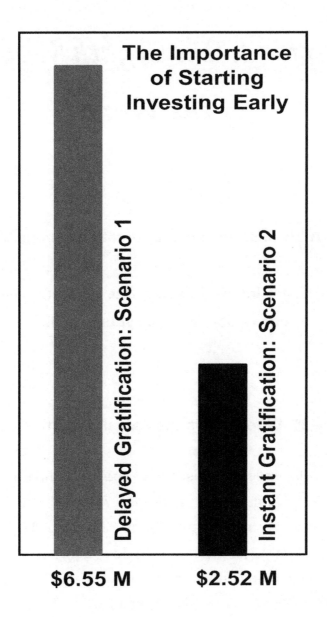

$6.55 M $2.52 M

You might be thinking: "Wow, I want to start investing as soon as possible. But how should I invest? What rate of return should I aim for?" This is discussed in the next chapter.

Chapter 4. The Eighth Wonder
of the World

Myth: **A 2% difference in rate of return is not a big deal.**

Money Tree: **Increasing your rate of return by just 2% can double or triple your wealth.**

1. A Mere 2% Difference in the Rate of Return

For illustrative purposes, assume that John's investment returns 10% annually in average. Amy is his next-door neighbor, and her investment returns 12% annually. There is a difference of only 2%. It is not a big deal, right?

Indeed, many people think this way: "A 2% difference is small and negligible. After all, it is just 2%."

For the purpose of illustration, assume that John and Amy both graduate from college and start working at the age of 22. They both work hard and save diligently. By the age of 30, they both have saved $100,000.

At the age of 30, John invests his $100,000 into an investment that returns 10% annually in average. Amy's is 12%. They both retire at the age of 67. From 30 to 67 is 37 years. How much does this $100,000 single investment become when they retire?

John: $100,000 x 1.10**37 = $3.4 million.
Amy: $100,000 x 1.12**37 = $6.6 million.

Important Point. A small, 2% difference in the rate of return, makes an extra $3.2 million for Amy.

This assumes that they sell 100% of their investments at the age of 67. Now, assume that, when they retire at 67, they have other means (such as cash savings, or cash from selling their big house and buying a small house, like many retirees do) to live on for 6 years. They do not need to sell their investments at the age of 67. Instead, they keep their investments till the age of 73. The difference between age 30 to age 73 is 43 years. How much does their initial $100,000 investment become when they are 73 years old?

John: $100,000 x 1.10**43 = $6.0 million.
Amy: $100,000 x 1.12**43 = $13.1 million.

First, do not be surprised by these big numbers. Due to inflation, they will be worth much less 43 years from now. Second, they may not be able to count on payments from social security by then. Third, after 43 years of medical and technological advances, people will be living significantly longer, and will need more money to support themselves and their loved ones living into their 80s, 90s and beyond. Therefore, they will need these large amounts of money.

Important Point. A small, 2% difference in the rate of return, makes an extra $7.1 million for Amy.

In the aforementioned simple illustration, they make a single investment of $100,000 at age 30, and then they do not put any more money into their investment. If they invest an additional $10,000 into their investment at age 31, then another $10,000 at age 32, and then $10,000 each year thereafter, the difference between the 10% and 12% rate of return would be even bigger than the aforementioned $7.1 million.

Important Point. A small difference in the rate of return is magnified to yield a big difference in wealth accumulation. Hence, we should strive to obtain a higher rate of return. Don't look down on, and neglect, a couple of percentages in the rate of return. It can produce millions of dollars of extra wealth to secure the financial freedom for us and for our loved ones.

2. A 10% Difference in the Rate of Return via Real Estate

As mentioned earlier, John invests at an average return of 10% annually. His neighbor across the street, Michael, loves houses and invests in rental houses. By using leverage, his average return is around 20% annually. As demonstrated with real-life deals in my first book *$5 Million in 8 Years: Real Estate Investing on the Side*, 20% annual return is quite achievable in real estate with an intelligent use of leverage. My wife and I obtained an average annual rate of 27% in our wealth growth, by spending only a few hours per week in real estate investing, as described in my first book.

For illustrative purposes, assume that John and Michael both invest $100,000 at the age of 30, and they sell at the age of 73. John's investment yields $6 million, as shown above.

Michael: $100,000 x 1.20**43 = $254 million.

You may be surprised by this big number. Most people would be. But as Wall Street would say: If you can achieve a 20% annual return year after year after year, eventually the whole world will be yours. This is the often-neglected power of earning a higher rate of return.

Important Point. From 10% to 20%, the annual rate of return is doubled. However, dramatically, the wealth accumulation is not just doubled from $6 million to $12 million. It is wonderfully increased by 42 folds, to $254 million.

3. A 5% Difference in Rate of Return via a Mixture of Real Estate and S&P 500

John's former classmate, Amanda, lives a few blocks

away. Amanda has also saved $100,000 by the age of 30. She invests part of it into an S&P 500 index fund. She invests the rest in real estate with leverage, like Michael.

The S&P 500 has returned approximately 10% annually in the past half a century. As stated in Chapter 1, the S&P 500 is used in this book as an example; the reader may use any other index fund or ETF that is similarly good. Just keep in mind that the S&P 500 beats 80-90% of all mutual funds and hedge funds in the long term.

Amanda's real estate investment returns about 20% annually, like Michael's. Her S&P 500 return is 10%. Assume that her overall average return is an intermediate 15% per year.

Let's compare John's investment with Amanda's. As shown above, by age 73, John's investment grows to $6 million.

Amanda: $100,000 x 1.15**43 = $40.7 million.

A small, 5% difference in the rate of return, yields $34.7 million extra money for Amanda.

Important Point. That's why compounding is called "the eighth wonder of the world". A small increase in the rate of return yields a huge, multi-million-dollar happy harvest for you.

I hope this chapter ignites your enthusiasm to maximize your return, which can earn you millions of dollars of additional wealth to achieve financial freedom.

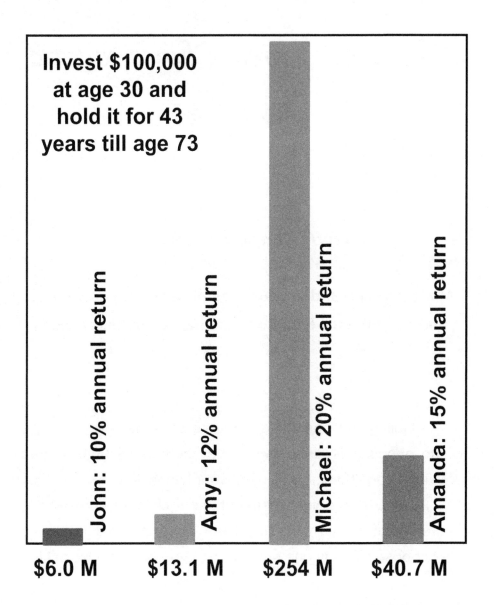

Invest $100,000 at age 30 and hold it for 43 years till age 73

John: 10% annual return — $6.0 M

Amy: 12% annual return — $13.1 M

Michael: 20% annual return — $254 M

Amanda: 15% annual return — $40.7 M

As you have seen in the preceding chapters, it is important to earn money to invest each year. Therefore, the next chapter discusses earning power and career choice.

Chapter 5. Career Choice toward Wealth

Myth: **Pursue your passion.**

Money Tree: **Bridge your passion with a lucrative field, and combine the two. Combination is wealth creation.**

College tuitions and dorm rents are expensive. "College is the opposite of kidnapping. They demand $100,000 from you; if you don't pay, they'll send your kid back."

College is a big investment in our children's career and future. What should they study and what career path should they choose? This is one of the most important choices in life.

1. Combination Is Creation

In 1986 and 1987, I was teaching physics in a university in China, and did research on the history of modern science. I published a dozen research papers in that field. One project involved investigation on how Japan succeeded in learning from the western countries and achieved fast modernization in science and technology in late 1800s and early 1900s, while China failed during the same time period. I went to libraries and read many historic documents. The purpose was to investigate why Japan succeeded, why China (the Qing Dynasty) failed a century ago, and what lessons could be learned for China to succeed in the modernization of science and technology.

One thing that caught my attention was a Japanese motto: "Combination is creation."

For example, they learned certain automobile technologies from the Unites States, and they learned some other technologies from Germany. Then they combined these technologies, and suddenly they were producing some of the best cars in the world.

They did not invent technology A. They did not invent technology B. But they combined the merits in A with the merits in B, and created a top-notch technology. This is the essence of the motto: "Combination is creation."

More recently, several years ago, I read the biography on the famous Steve Jobs, and noticed that he employed the "combination is creation" approach too. He did not call it this name, but he said that he focused on the intersection between art and technology. He had a strong artistic instinct, and he combined that competitive edge with technology. In addition, he advised the young generation to focus on the intersection between computer technology and biology and medicine.

2. Combining Physics with Finance

When children grow up and are ready to choose a career path, they face one of the most important choices in their lives.

He or she has a passion, a personal interest. However, he or she also faces the need to be able to make a living, support a family, and have a good quality of life.

If that passion happens to be in computer science or medicine or other fields where jobs are available and salaries are good, then the choice is easy.

However, often, the passion is in a field where jobs are hard to find and salaries are relatively low. Then the choice becomes difficult. Should the young person pursue his or her passion, and live a financially insecure life? Or, should they study something that pays well, but sacrifice their passion?

This is where "combination is creation" becomes useful.

I have a friend who obtained a PhD degree in nuclear physics. It involved a lot of theoretical calculations and computer modeling. Nuclear physicists may find jobs in the Unites States national labs, where they work as postdoctoral researchers first, with a typical salary of $40,000 to $50,000. After 2-3 years, if the postdoctor's performance is excellent, he or she is then hired as a regular employee.

Another option is that, after 2-3 years of postdoctoral training, he or she can apply to become a professor in a university. A typical tenure-track assistant professor position in physics often draws hundreds of applicants. Six of the best applicants are selected for the first interview. Of those, three are then selected for the second interview, and then the best one is hired. The tenure-track assistant professor needs to work really hard and perform really well in order to get tenured; otherwise, at the end of the six years, he or she will be let go. Their annual salaries are typically around $70,000 to $100,000.

Instead of choosing one of these routes, my nuclear physicist friend went to Wall Street and found a job, where he combined his physics modeling and computer skills with finance and investing. He did not have to work as a postdoctor for 2-3 years, and his salary was three times that of a physics assistant professor. After working for investment firms for two decades, he quit his job and opened his own mutual fund company. He developed computer models for selecting companies and investing in the stock market. Some big clients have given him significant amounts of money to invest, and he has been doing well.

Not only is he making a lot of money, but he also has a lot of freedom. Once his mutual fund company is up and running and the computer models are being executed, he has a lot of time for himself. He and I are on the same exercise app that tracks how many steps we have walked or run daily. His daily number has been routinely above 20,000 steps/day.

Therefore, combining his physics and computer training with finance and investing has served him well. Indeed, combination is creation. For him, it has created wealth, career achievements and satisfaction, and time to enjoy life.

3. A Bigger Example

James Simons was born in 1938 in Brookline, Massachusetts. When he was 14 years old, he worked as a floor sweeper at a garden supply store. Later, he studied math and obtained his PhD degree, eventually becoming the chairman of the mathematics department at the State University of New York at Stony Brook. While at Stony Brook, he encountered a friend who invested money in a company. The amount of money that friend made in a short 8 months was 10 times the total wealth that Prof. Simons had.

This served as a trigger for the highly-intelligent but lowly-paid mathematician. Prof. Simons decided to quit his job and start investing. In 1978, he started his hedge fund Monemetrics. In 1982, when he was 44 years old, he founded the investment company Renaissance Technologies.

Prof. Simons became a major example of "combination is creation". He combined math and computer modeling with investing. He developed quantitative analyses, for which he was later crowned "The Quant King".

The Quant King combined mathematics, data analysis and other scientific methods with finance and investments. He hired programmers, mathematicians and physicists for his investment company. The company thrived, making him the 24th-richest person in the United States, with a net asset of $23.5 billion, as of 10/26/2020.[1] The Quant King was ranked on the Forbes 2019 list as being the number 1 highest-earner among all hedge fund managers. In addition, he became a philanthropist and has been giving away billions to charities.

None of this would have been possible if he had stayed with math alone, and had not combined math with investing.

Therefore, in this example, the power of combination-is-creation has created billions of dollars for Dr. Simons, hundreds of jobs in his company, and billions of dollars for charities.

4. My Friend's Son

Jay is my son Darnell's best friend. They grew up in the church together. They celebrate birthday parties and travel together. My wife and I are friends with Jay's parents. Jay is very good at math. Math was his major in college.

While Jay was in college, one day, I met with him for lunch. We chatted about my small investing experience. I also told him about Prof. James Simons who was a mathematician-turned-investor and billionaire. I suggested to Jay that instead of pursuing pure math as a career, that he might consider taking a few classes in finance, and combine math with finance. In addition, I asked my wife to send an article about James Simons to Jay's mother to let her and Jay both read it.

After graduation, Jay started working for an investment company on Wall Street. Jay's salary plus bonus approached $300,000, according to Darnell. That's very good for a young mathematician with just a bachelor's degree. And he did not have to sacrifice his math passion to go to a medical school, a dental school or a law school. Instead, he gets to continue to pursue his math passion and make full use of his talents and gifts, by combining math with investing.

I am not trying to take any credit for Jay's success. He is outstanding and deserves all the credit. My purpose of using his example is to show that it fits "Combination is creation."

5. My Daughter's High-School College Application and Selecting a Career in College

When my daughter Joyce was in high school and getting ready for her college application, she had a hard time deciding what major to study in college and what career to pursue.

She has always loved reading and writing. She reads books after books. She has won awards in many writing competitions. Her math and science are also excellent, which actually made it more difficult for her to decide what direction to pursue as her career.

We sent her to a bioengineering lab to be a summer intern. She did very well and everyone there loved her. However, she told my wife and I that she did not want to be a medical doctor, nor a dentist, nor a pharmacist. In addition, she did not want to study science or engineering. She did not want to study computer either. She was good at these subjects. She was a straight-A student in an excellent high school, and was among the top 10% in her class. However, it's just that she did not have the passion to do these things as a life-long career.

Eventually, Joyce decided to go to business school because that could combine her excellent reading, writing, expression and presentation, and math skills.

While in college, she worked as a summer intern in an accounting department. She found that the work suited her quite well. She won high praises from her supervisor. She did so well that the colleagues kept asking her to go back.

She is good at math and computer, and she is calm, responsible, careful and meticulous. So, she thinks that she can become a CPA (certified public accountant) and do accounting as her career.

I said: "Sure, accounting suits your skills and personality well. But, how about your passion for language and writing?"

Joyce thought for a moment: "I can always do writing as a hobby."

I tried to give her some advice: "Sure. Maybe someday you can combine your business and accounting training with writing. One possibility is that you may write biographies of people like Zuckerburg, Musk, Jack Ma, etc. Most writers graduating from English departments do not have your business training and accounting insights. You are being trained in a business school. You will become a CPA. So you can study these successful business people and teach others on how to be successful. Yes, it takes time. It may take you a year to do research and write a book about a billionaire. But if your book can help a lot of people to learn how to be successful, then it is meaningful. And if your book sells, say, 100,000 copies, and you make $3 per copy, then you make $300,000 per book. Once you finish a book, then you can take a vacation in Europe for a month. Then you start to do research on another billionaire and write another book."

My beautiful darling had twinkles in her big pretty eyes: "Sounds very interesting. I do love writing and the freedom to set my own schedules. I will definitely think about this."

I emphasized: "Please do. This could combine your business training with your writing passion. It is advantageous to bridge your passion with a neighboring lucrative field, and combine the two. That way, you get to pursue your passion without compromising your income and quality of life."

6. My Colleague's Daughter

I have a colleague Sholto, a first-generation immigrant from Japan, and a PhD research scientist. His daughter Sherry was born in the United States, but her parents had her learn the Japanese language on the side while growing up in the United States. Her English is excellent, and her Japanese is also good. Sherry graduated from law school focusing on intellectual property law, and joined a law firm in a big city.

Because Sherry knew English, Japanese and intellectual property law, she became indispensable to the law firm dealing with global companies doing business in both the United States and Japan. After only a few years, her annual salary and bonus exceeded $400,000.

Sholto told me with a mixed sweet and sour tone: "I am happy for Sherry that she is doing so well. But it also makes me feel sad that I've been working in the wrong field: a hard-working scientist in his 50s, earning only a quarter of what his young daughter is earning."

Indeed, the combination of Sherry's expertise in intellectual property law, English, and Japanese served her well. She told Sholto that in the law field, people with combined expertise earned significantly more. For example, if you study intellectual property law but also have a degree in engineering, you could become an important partner in a law firm that focuses on intellectual properties of engineering companies and technology companies.

Or, if your undergraduate degree is in chemistry or biology, and then you go to law school to study intellectual property law, you could do very well focusing on intellectual properties of drug manufacturers and biotech companies.

Indeed, combination is creation. It will create wealth for you by not only having a great earning power, but also by investing a portion of your larger salary in the compounding magic machine, as the other chapters of this book demonstrate.

7. Your Passion Is Fulfilled via Financial Freedom, Time Freedom and Life Freedom

Therefore, it pays to bridge your passion with a lucrative field, and combine your passion with that field. You will experience that "combination is creation". It will create wealth for you and your loved ones.

The aforementioned examples will help you consider your own unique combinations, based on your own situation. Perhaps you would combine biology with computer science. Perhaps you would combine medicine with big data. Perhaps you would combine the study of the human body with engineering. Or music with technology. Or art with technology. Or an MBA degree with sports. Or a law degree with real estate investing. Or the knowledge of history with public speaking and political science. Or writing with marketing, etc.

I hope this chapter will open your eyes to the vast possibilities of combinations to create more wealth and opportunities for you. This chapter helps you to focus not only on (1) your passion and interest, but also (2) earning a decent income and supporting your family, as well as (3) quality of life and financial freedom for yourself and your loved ones.

We work hard to pursue happiness in our lives. Freedom, liberty, and the pursuit of happiness are our human rights. The combination-is-creation approach will bring benefits to your career and earning power. This, combined with the investing methods described in this book, will help you reach your financial freedom.

Financial freedom enables and facilitates you to pursue your passion. Once you achieve your financial freedom, then you have time to pursue your passion and your interests. You have the option to retire early. You have time to sleep in. You have time to take a long vacation in Europe or Asia. You have time to spend on music, dance, sports, volunteering, etc. You have time to spend with your family and friends.

Financial freedom brings you the life freedom. For example, if your company treats you unfairly, you can afford to quit and not put up with the stress and anxiety because you need the paychecks to make a living. If you have a nasty boss, you can fire your boss and quit your job. How to live your life is decided by you. It is not decided by your boss, your company, or the pressure and need to put food on the table.

Therefore, it takes financial freedom to truly pursue your passion, without sacrificing the quality of life or worrying about money. The combination-is-creation method will provide the financial security to enable you to truly pursue your passion.

Among the three types of freedom (financial freedom, time freedom, life freedom), financial freedom is the foundation. And the combination-is-creation method, along with the other investing methods in this book, will help you to achieve these three types of freedom.

Important Point. The combination-is-creation method does not mean to sacrifice your passion. Quite the contrary, it helps fulfill your passion. The combination-is-creation approach in your career leads to financial freedom, which in turn leads to time freedom and life freedom. They provide the financial resources and time to pursue your passion, be it dancing, painting, music, sports, or volunteering.

Total Salary in One's Working Life in 35 Years

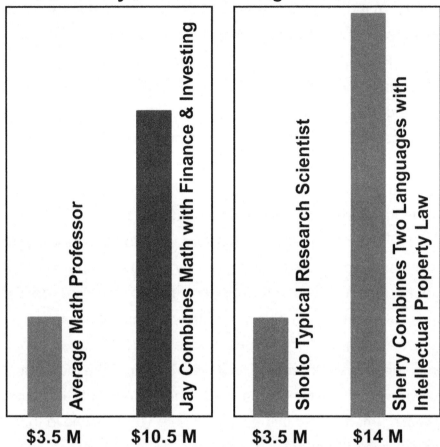

| $3.5 M | $10.5 M | $3.5 M | $14 M |

To illustrate the point, this chart makes the following assumptions. (1) A typical salary of $100,000 for an average math professor. (2) A typical salary of $100,000 for Sholto as a PhD scientist. (3) Jay's salary is $300,000, and Sherry's salary is $400,000. (3) Assume that they all work for 35 years and then retire, without annual increases in salary (to keep the math simple). M = million.

This chart shows that, compared to a math professor, combining math with finance for Jay would make $7 million more in his career. Compared to a research scientist, combining intellectual property law with languages for Sherry would make $10 million more in her career.

This chart includes salary income only, without including the investments. They use a portion of the salary to invest over the years. Earning a higher salary enables one to have more money to invest every year. These investments grow by the magic compounding over time, and will eventually far exceed the salary-earning power itself. Therefore, the differences will be even bigger than what is shown in this chart.

Summary. To the young generation, to parents and mentors who are trying to guide the young, and to all people who are faced with a career choice: Make an effort to combine your passion and talent with an important and lucrative field. Combination is creation. This enables you to contribute to the society in a maximal way by combining your passion/talent with an important trend and opportunity. This creates a satisfying and fulfilling career for you. This creates success and happiness. This creates wealth for you and for your loved ones.

Besides using the combination-is-creation method to earn a good salary, another important way to grow wealth is to buy a house, which the next chapter focuses on.

Chapter 6. The Joy of Home Ownership

Myth: **You should rent and not buy a house unless you will stay in the house for at least 5 years.**

Money Tree: **Analyze case by case. Even 2-3 years of living in the house often yields substantial profits.**

This chapter is for the young professionals who may be looking to buy a house soon, for parents who have young professional children and want to help guide them into homeownership, for parents who have college kids who will start working soon, and for anyone who is debating whether to buy a house or to rent.

Home sweet home!

Indeed, home is where the heart is, and there is no place like home. As Andre Rieu said: "Coming home is one of the most beautiful things."[1]

The house is not only the place of enjoyment, but also an important investment for ordinary people.

1. Are Debt and Mortgages Good or Bad?

Well-known movie actor Will Smith said: "Too many people spend money they haven't earned, to buy things they don't want, to impress people they don't like."[2] "Spending money they haven't earned" means taking on debt, and this can get them into financial trouble.

To correct such mistakes, some people have gone from one extreme to the other extreme. There have been a lot of talk and promotion about "debt-free living", "live a debt-free life", and "the benefits of no debt".

Some people claim: "No mortgage, no debt, no stress!"

Others declare: "Being debt-free is the new rich!"

Sure, a young professional may choose to rent an apartment or a house, and live a mortgage-free and debt-free life.

Alternatively, in the case of someone with a relatively stable job, s/he may buy a condo or a house with a mortgage. However, that means debt. So:

"Is debt good or bad?"

A knife is bad when it is used to hurt someone.

A knife is good when it is used to prepare food to feed someone.

Some debts are bad. For example, someone borrows money from his or her credit card, at an interest rate of 19%, to buy fancy shoes and clothes. Or, a couple, who lives from paycheck to paycheck, takes a loan to buy a boat that depreciates over time. In addition, the boat costs money for repairs and maintenance.

However, some debts are good, as shown below.

2. Benefits of Buying versus Renting

My daughter Sweetie and her husband Moutai had been working and renting a one-bedroom apartment in a big city in the United States in 2017 and 2018. Their rent was $2,200/month, plus $200/month for a spot to park their car in the underground garage below their apartment building.

So, their total rent payment was $2,400/month. They lived there for two years.

Then, they adopted a dog from a shelter, and decided to buy a house with more space and a yard. In the spring of 2019, they moved into their house. It's a new townhouse in the suburb of the same city where they rented. This townhouse has three bedrooms and three full bathrooms, with 2,200 square feet of space, a garage, and a rooftop deck. It was the rooftop deck that attracted Sweetie and Moutai to choose this house, as they would love to have parties with friends on the rooftop deck.

The price for this townhouse was $400,000. They made a down payment of 20%, and the rest ($320,000) was a mortgage from a bank. They recently refinanced to a low interest rate of 3%, for a 30-year fixed mortgage.

Their monthly mortgage payment is about $1,700. Their principal + interest payment is $1,349/month. The rest includes insurance and property tax. The interest is ($320,000 x 0.03)/12 = $800/month. The principal payment = $1,349 - $800 = $549.

Barbeque on the rooftop deck of the new house of Sweetie and Moutai

The principal is paid into their own pocket, because it reduces the money that they owe the bank. In addition, the interest and property tax payments are tax-deductible. Compared to paying rent which is not tax-deductible, they save in tax deductions to the effect of about $250/month.

Therefore, their effective monthly payment for this house is $1,700 - $549 (principal which is paid to themselves) - $250 (in tax savings) = $901/month.

This means that they save $1,499, compared to their previous $2,400 monthly rent ($2,400 - $901 = $1,499).

Even factoring in the higher utility bills due to the larger space and the repairs and maintenance costs (which are minimal because this is a new house), they still save more than $1,000/month, compared to renting.

As of writing this in fall 2020, they had lived in their house for 20 months. This means saving at least $1,000 x 20 months = $20,000, compared to their previous rent payments.

Furthermore, another benefit of ownership of this house is appreciation. When they lived in the apartment building for two years, if the building value increased by 8% (simply assuming 4% appreciation per year to illustrate the point), that 8% increase in value belonged to the owner of the building. Renters pay rent each month but share nothing in the building's appreciation in value.

In fall 2020, similar townhouses were selling for about $440,000 to $450,000 in Sweetie's neighborhood. Therefore, they had made at least $40,000 in price appreciation in their house. Here is a conservative estimate of the extra money they made in just 20 months, compared to renting:

$20,000 (savings compared to renting) + $40,000 (house appreciation) = $60,000.

This is a good profit for the young couple in just 20

months, compared to renting. In addition, they have been enjoying the spacious new house with their dog. Their enjoyment and happiness are precious and priceless.

3. Drawbacks in Buying a House

However, there are several drawbacks in buying a house. First, looking at houses, negotiations, paperwork, etc., take time and effort (although one does learn a lot in this process, so this is experience gained, not time wasted).

Second, for such a townhouse, there is about $13,000 closing costs when you buy it. Then when you sell it, you pay another $13,000 in closing costs. Closing costs depend on the settlement company and your location, as transfer taxes and other fees differ from place to place. Your real estate agent should be able to give you an estimate on the closing costs.

Third, once you are a homeowner for several years, if you have to sell the house, you, being the seller, have to pay 4-6% in commission to the real estate agents. Some discount agents charge 1.5% to list the house as the seller's agent, and then pay the buyer's agent 2.5%, for a total of 4%. Some sellers pay 5%, and some sellers pay 6%.

Fourth, there is the risk of buying into a bubble, and then the price declines in the next several years when you have to sell the house at a loss. The 2008-2009 crash was one of the worst in a century, and such a major housing bubble/bust is rare in a lifetime. Therefore, most of the times, buying a house with leverage is a lucrative investment; just make sure that you have safeguards in place. For the use of caution and safeguards in investing, please see Chapter 21.

These are the main reasons why people avoid buying a house and then having to sell it soon. Of course, there are other reasons too, such as job security, family situation, and personal preference regarding whether to rent or to buy.

4. A Home-Buying Myth

Here is a popular myth: "If you buy a house, you have to live in the house for at least five years to make financial sense."

If you buy a house and live in it for 5 to 10 years or longer, that's great. However, often, people relocate due to job changes, family issues and other reasons. If they could stay in one place for only 3-4 years, should they avoid buying a house?

I have done analyses of many houses and found that this myth is untrue. Instead, we should analyze case by case.

For example, in the case of Sweetie and Moutai, assume that they live in their house for only two years, which is well short of the five years according to the myth. Assume that after two years, they for some reason have to sell their house.

Their costs are: $13,000 (closing costs when they buy) + $13,000 (closing costs when they sell) + 4% commission x $440,000 (house price when they sell it) = $43,600.

Their savings from monthly payments, compared to their previous renting, were at least $1,000/month, as described above. Therefore, in two years, they save at least $1,000 x 24 months = $24,000, compared to their previous renting.

Regarding house value appreciation, their house value at sale ($440,000) - $400,000 purchase price = $40,000.

Therefore, in two years, $24,000 + $40,000 = $64,000.

This minus their closing costs and agent commission = $64,000 - $43,600 = $20,400.

Therefore, even if they live in this house for only two years and then sell this house, they would still gain a net profit of $20,400 that goes into their pocket.

This is in addition to gaining valuable experience with buying and selling a house, enjoying the large space with their dog, and happiness of parties with friends on the rooftop deck.

Important Point. Therefore, "you have to stay in the house for at least five years to be profitable" is a myth and not true. The right way should be "case by case" analysis. Otherwise, you would lose money in rent payments, let go tens of thousands of dollars in net profits, lose the enjoyment of a larger space and the pride of home ownership, and miss the valuable opportunity to learn about buying and selling a house. The latter could help lay the foundation for real estate investing if one chooses to go in that direction.

Furthermore, if Sweetie and Moutai live in this house for more than two years (and they do plan to stay for many more years), their net profit would be much greater, as shown below.

Let's estimate their net profit if they stay for 5 years.

Their savings from monthly payments, compared to their previous renting, are $1,000/month, as described above. In 5 years, they save $1,000 x 60 months = $60,000.

House value appreciation (assuming 4% appreciation annually) = $400,000 x 1.04**5 - $400,000 = $86,661.

Their net profit in 5 years = $60,000 (savings) + $86,661 (appreciation) - $45,466 (closing, 4% agent costs) = $101,195.

5. Don't Let the Myth Cost You Big Bucks

The reason I emphasize this point is that this myth "you have to stay in the house for five years to make financial sense" has stopped a lot of people from buying a house.

Nowadays, many people cannot guarantee a job stability in one location for longer than five years. And this myth has scared them from buying a house.

However, many people can see reasonably well, by looking at the business of the company and talking to their bosses, that they will be able to keep their job in the same location for, say, 3 or 4 years. Maybe they cannot plan for more than 5 years. But they can reasonably well plan for 3 or 4 years.

Then, instead of being stopped by this myth, they should analyze. They can look at the math in this chapter, instead of blindly believing: "I can see a job stability for 3 or 4 years. It is unclear beyond that. So, I will forget about buying a house."

Of course, people are different. Some simply prefer to rent and not buy a house. That is fine, as long as it is based on their own preference, and not based on believing the myth.

The Harm of This Myth. This myth has inhibited numerous people from homeownership, cost them tens of thousands of dollars in housing price appreciation and tax benefits, and robbed them of the enjoyment and pride of having a house of their own. If you are currently a renter, I hope this chapter will help you to analyze and make a better decision.

In Sweetie's case, buying a house and living there for just two years was enough to not only break even, but also yield a decent net profit, than renting.

Of course, they do plan to stay in their house for many more years. And their profit will grow, while they enjoy this house over the years.

For example, let's look at 10 years. Assume a 4% housing value appreciation which is close to the long-term national historic average in the United States. In 10 years, their house will be worth ($400,000 x 1.04**10 =) $592,098. Meanwhile, they will owe less and less money to their lender, because they are paying down their loan every month.

Here is a review on how to calculate the appreciation in value. Do not be scared by the numbers. This is easy and useful math, and will be a beneficial tool for you if you want to invest to achieve financial freedom.

$400,000 appreciating at 4% annually becomes: $400,000 x 1.04 = $416,000 after one year.

After two years, it becomes: $400,000 x 1.04 x 1.04 =

$432,640.

After 5 years, it becomes: $400,000 x 1.04 x 1.04 x 1.04 x 1.04 x 1.04 = $486,661.

After 10 years, it becomes: $400,000 x 1.04**10 = $592,098.

Important Point. (1) In ten years, they save at least $120,000 in monthly payments (as aforementioned, when compared to paying rent and parking fees, they save at least $1,000 per month by owning their house and paying their mortgage with tax benefits on the interest payments). (2) In ten years, they will build an equity of more than $300,000 in their house. (3) Renting will give them 0 equity.

Money Tree. Sweetie's house is like a money tree that grows more and more money for them over time. If you are a renter, I hope this chapter will bring your substantial benefits.

Sweetie said that emotionally, it took courage and boldness to go ahead and borrow $320,000 from the bank to buy this house. They had never borrowed money before, and this was a large amount for the young couple.

However, as people say: "Fortune favors the bold."

Of course, besides being bold, home buyers also need to use caution and safeguards. They need to know how and what to buy, understand the local market because all real estate is local, and learn effective negotiation skills to get the best possible deal. These important topics are covered in my first book *$5 Million in 8 Years: Real Estate Investing on the Side*, and are not repeated here.

6. Summary

(1) For Sweetie and Moutai, by buying their house, they save money every month, compared to their previous rents.

(2) Their interest payments are tax deductible.

(3) They have a lot more space to enjoy with their dog and a roof-top deck to entertain friends. The enjoyment and home ownership pride are priceless.

(4) The myth "if you buy a house, you have to stay for 5 years to be profitable" is not true. The right way is "case by case analysis". Often, 3 or 4 or even 2 years are enough to yield a decent net profit, compared to renting. In addition, going through, and learning about, the house-buying process helps lay a foundation for their future investing.

(5) Sweetie and Moutai are growing a money tree with appreciation and principal reduction. This will yield more than $300,000 in equity in ten years. Renting has 0 equity.

This chapter demonstrates the substantial benefits of homeownership, with the example of Sweetie and Moutai, who bought their house using a mortgage. Should they prepay their mortgage to pay it off early? This issue is discussed in the next chapter.

Chapter 7. A Mortgage-Free Life Costs You Millions

Myth: Prepay and pay off your mortgage, then live mortgage-free.

Money Tree: Use your house as the "mother" tree to breed more money trees.

Gaston Bachelard, the French philosopher, said: "If I were asked to name the chief benefit of the house, I should say: the house shelters day-dreamers, the house protects the dreamer, and the house allows one to dream in peace."[1]

We all have our dreams. It's good to be a dreamer. America is still one of the best places on earth for the dreamer, providing the conditions for one to succeed with upward mobility. My wife and I are living proof of the American dream.

This chapter will demonstrate that the house not only shelters the day-dreamer, but also enables one to actually realize the dream of financial freedom.

This chapter shows simple methods to make millions. If you are willing to spend half an hour to read this chapter thoroughly, it could make a difference of millions of dollars in your life.

Many people got burned by bad debts, for example, through the irresponsible lending in 2005-2006, as well as high-interest credit card debts. As a result, many have gone from one extreme to the other extreme.

It is now popular to promote myths such as "debt-free living", and encourage the prepaying of the mortgage, to pay it off as early as possible.

As mentioned in the last chapter, my daughter Sweetie and her husband Moutai bought a house for $400,000, when Sweetie was 24 and Moutai was 26, in early spring 2019.

Sweetie and Moutai have a 30-year mortgage, and if they follow this book, they likely will do cash-out refinances in the future years to maintain their leverage and grow their wealth, and not pay off their mortgage early.

However, for illustrative purposes, assume that they go with the prepaying trend, and pay off their mortgage early, in 15 years, instead of 30 years.

Fifteen years from 2019 would be 2034 (when Sweetie is 39). Assume that the house value appreciates by 4% annually, similar to the long-term national average in the United States. Then in 2034, their house value will be $400,000 x 1.04**15 = $720,377.

As mentioned above, they would pay off their mortgage

by 2034. Hence, in 2034, the equity in their house would be $720,377.

The following are three different methods. The differences are night and day.

1. Method 1 - Fear of Debt

As mentioned above, by 2034, Sweetie and Moutai have paid off their mortgage. Their house value = $720,377. Then from 2034 to 2062, they live in this house mortgage-free.

Assume that Sweetie retires in 2062 at the age of 67. From 2034 to 2062 is 28 years. The house value is $720,377 in 2034. Assume that the house continues to appreciate by 4% annually. Then, in 2062, the house value becomes: $720,377 x $1.04**28$ = $2.2 million.

Do not be surprised by the big number of $2.2 million. Due to inflation, the $2.2 million in 2062 will be worth much less than the $2.2 million now.

Therefore, using the debt-free method, they will have $2.2 million from this house in 2062.

2. Method 2 - Use Equity in the House as the "Mother" Tree to Breed More Money Trees: Use "Good Debt" to Buy Rental Properties

In 2034, they pay off the mortgage, and have an equity of $720,377 in their house, the same as Method 1.

However, in Method 2, instead of mortgage-free, they do a cash-out refinance in 2034 and pull out $500,000 of cash.

They use this cash to make the 20% down payment to buy several rental houses, with 80% loans from the banks. They use the rental income to pay the mortgages and maintenance costs.

This will enable their invested money ($500,000) to grow at around 20% annual rate of return. The use of leverage can achieve a rate of return of around 25%, even if the house appreciation is only 4% annually. This was demonstrated in my book *$5 Million in 8 Years: Real Estate Investing on the Side*. Of course, borrowing money to buy rental properties have to follow safeguards to minimize risks, which are discussed in my first book.

Below is a brief checklist of safeguards for loans.

(1) Avoid over-leveraging. While the banks nowadays do not freely give out loans anymore like they did in 2005, the small investor should still have individual analyses and self-control to avoid the foreclosures that happened in 2008-2009.

(2) Avoid bad loans, e.g., credit-card loans to buy a boat.

(3) Make sure that you have made preparations and have reserves to pay the mortgages on loans. In my case, besides salaries, we have more than $100,000/year positive cash flow after paying all the mortgages and other expenses.

(4) Make at least 20% down payment when buying a rental property. All our properties were purchased with at least

20% down payment, sometimes with 25%, 30%, or more.

(5) My wife and I have several properties with a lot of equity in them. For example, we currently have several townhouses with more than $200,000 equity in each house. In the rare case that our more than $100,000 cash flow disappears (which is highly unlikely) and we need cash to pay the mortgages, we can sell one of these townhouses to raise cash. I don't see that happening, but it's better to have several layers of safeguards in place, just in case.

As long as they follow these safeguards, when their rental houses have accumulated more equity after several years, they can repeat the cash-out refinance. They can pull out more cash to use as down-payments to buy more rental properties. Their money trees continue to breed more baby money trees. In this way, they maintain a healthy leverage in their properties, thereby maintaining the approximately 20% annual rate of return.

From 2034 to 2062 is 28 years. The $500,000, growing at about 20% annually, becomes by 2062:

$500,000 x 1.2**28 = $82.4 million.

In addition, they still have their first house which has increased in value to $2.2 million, as shown in Method 1.

Therefore, in Method 2, when Sweetie retires in 2062, they have $84.6 million.

In this way, they effectively turn the stones and bricks of their house into gold.

This is a simple illustration to avoid complicated math. In reality, instead of taking out $500,000 equity in 2034 and buying a bunch of rental properties in the same year, they could do a cash-out refinance every few years, starting before 2034. For example, they could do a cash-out refinance on their primary residence in 2025 and use the cash to buy rental properties. Then by 2030, they would have more equity in their primary residence due to price appreciation and principal reduction from paying the mortgages every month. So, they could do another cash-out refinance in 2030 and use the cash to buy rental properties. Then they repeat it again in 2035 on their primary residence. Furthermore, after several years of equity accumulation, they can do cash-out refinances on their rental properties (baby trees growing up) and use the pulled-out cash to buy more rental properties (grandkids money trees).

3. Method 3 - Use Equity in the House as the "Mother" Tree to Breed More Money Trees: Use "Good Debt" to Invest in the S&P 500

In this example, assume that Sweetie and Moutai do not want to deal with rental properties. As mentioned above, in 2034, they pay off the mortgage in their house. They do a cash-out refinance and pull out $500,000 cash. Then they pour this $500,000 into an index fund (such as the S&P 500). Then they forget about it. The S&P 500 beats most busy and stressful day-traders, and beats most mutual funds and hedge funds.

In the short term, the S&P 500 is volatile. However, in the long term, from 1965-2020, with dividend reinvested, the S&P 500 has returned an average of 10% annually.

This $500,000, growing at 10% annually from 2034 to 2062, becomes:

$500,000 x 1.1**28 = $7.2 million.

In addition, they still have their house which has increased in value to $2.2 million, as shown in Method 1.

Therefore, using Method 3, in 2062 when Sweetie retires, they will have $9.4 million.

This is a simple illustration. In reality, instead of taking out $500,000 equity in 2034 and dumping it into the S&P 500 at once, they should do a cash-out refinance every few years, and buy the S&P 500 via dollar cost averaging. For example, they could do a cash-out refinance in 2025, then in 2030, then in 2035, etc. Each time, they would pour the cash into the S&P 500. Their results would be even better than the $7.2 million above, because they start investing in the S&P 500 in 2025, instead of 2034. Using this simple Method 3, they will have millions of dollars more than Method 1.

4. Huge Benefits of "Good Debt"

Of course, in Methods 2 and 3, they would need to pay a monthly mortgage on the $500,000 refinance loan that they take out of their house. They would need to pay property tax and insurance on their house no matter what, even in Method

1. Hence, the difference is that they need to pay the principal and interest on the $500,000 loan in Methods 2 and 3. However, the principal is paid into their own pocket, because it reduces the loan that they owe the bank. Depending on whether they use a 15-year-fixed or 30-year-fixed mortgage for this $500,000, in either case their interest payment to the bank will be less than $1 million in the 28 years from 2034 to 2062. Therefore, for Method 3,

9.4 million (Method 3) - 1 million (interest payments) - 2.2 million (Method 1) = 6.2 million.

Methods 3 earns $6.2 million more than Method 1.

In addition, this interest payment is tax-deductible. In contrast, there is no interest to help reduce their taxes in Method 1. Some details are not included in the math here, in order to illustrate the important point without inundating the reader with too much detailed math. For example, investments have tax issues; please contact an accountant for tax issues.

Benefit of Method 2. Therefore, in Method 2, they make more than $80 million extra money, compared to Method 1.

Benefit of Method 3. Even in the example of Method 3 which uses the trouble-free and passive S&P 500, they still make $6.2 million extra money, compared to Method 1.

Important Point. Therefore, the conventional wisdom of "Prepay and pay off your mortgage early. Live a mortgage-free

81

life" can rob an ordinary family millions of dollars. It has damaged the financial security for numerous families.

5. What Do Most Homeowners Do? They Lose Millions That Otherwise Would Have Been Theirs

This chapter uses Sweetie and Moutai as an example. They have read this and found it helpful, and they will reference this chapter in their future planning.

The purpose of this chapter, though, is to help numerous other homeowners too.

Unfortunately, most homeowners that I know of choose Method 1. Many hardworking people that I know use Method 1. Years ago, a couple gave me a brochure describing how to prepay and pay off the home mortgage fast, in order to live mortgage-free.

In February 2020, another good friend told me that she and her husband had been prepaying their home mortgage and they were almost done with it, and after that, they would live a debt-free life.

These hardworking people diligently prepay their mortgages in order to pay them off early. Then they have a mortgage-free house, with a lot of equity sitting in the house doing nothing. In this process, they lose the opportunity to acquire substantial amounts of wealth for the financial security of themselves and for their loved ones.

6. Turn Stones into Gold

Methods 2 and 3 require the intelligent use of leverage to grow money trees. Even though the math makes sense, it still takes courage to take out a loan to invest, whether the loan amount is $200,000 or $1 million. Courage is needed on the road to financial freedom. Indeed, as the Greek philosopher Thucydides said:

"The secret to happiness is freedom... And the secret to freedom is courage."[2]

For Method 2, as shown in my first book,[3] even if you have a full-time job, real estate investing can be done on the side. By using other people's time and talents, real estate investing takes me only two to four hours per week of my time. It takes less time than what other people spend on the internet or watching TV.

Even if some people do not want to use Method 2, at the very least, they should consider Method 3. This passive, "do-nothing" S&P 500 method can still make $6.2 million more than the conventional wisdom Method 1.

So, what is stopping people from using Method 3?

Some people ask: "What if I do a cash-out refinance and put the money into the S&P 500, and then it crashes by 30%?"

I use two weapons to kill the risk. (1) I would do cash-out refinances every year, or very couple of years, and put the cash into the S&P 500 over time for dollar cost averaging. (2) I would hold the S&P 500 for the long term. If I hold it for only a year, it could drop significantly. However, if I do dollar cost averaging, and hold it for, say, 15 years, I should be fine.

Turn stones and bricks of your house and rentals into gold

In addition, you do not have to wait till you pay off your mortgage to start using Methods 2 and 3. If your house value is $500,000, and you still owe the bank $150,000, you can start the cash-out refinance to use Methods 2 and 3. The earlier we start, the better, due the magic effect of compounding, as shown in Chapter 3. This can be especially beneficial if we can lock in a low interest rate in the refinance, to turn the stones and bricks of our house and rental properties into gold.

Of course, if you are retired and say, 70 years old, I am not suggesting that you do cash-out refinances and invest in the S&P 500. This is because you may not want to hold it for 10 or 15 years. However, for the numerous homeowners who are in their 30s, 40s and 50s, this is a simple, although think-outside-of-the-box, way to grow substantial wealth and achieve financial freedom.

7. Are You Willing to Leave the Crowd and Take the Less-Traveled Path?

The traditional and popular Method 1 makes many families lose millions of dollars that otherwise would have been theirs to enjoy life with their loved ones.

Self-made millionaires are a small minority group among the entire population. Therefore, if we want to be wealthy, we have to be in the minority. We cannot go with the herd. We have to have independent thinking.

As the investment legend John Templeton advised:

"It is impossible to produce superior performance unless you do something different from the majority."[4]

While most people think inside the box, we need to think outside of the box. When they say: "Debt-free is stress-free!

Debt is dangerous!" We have to have the guts to go against the crowd. We have to think independently, instead of blindly believing the conventional wisdom. We have to rise above the herd noise, focus on the numbers, and calmly analyze.

Do the math, do the due diligence, then be willing to leave the crowd, and take the less-traveled path. Because: Only a small number of people become self-made millionaires.

8. Summary

The fear of debt can cost homeowners substantial amounts of money, in many cases make them lose millions of dollars. In contrast, as shown in Methods 2 and 3, making use of "good debt" from the equity in our house can earn millions.

Method 2 makes $80 million extra money, and Method 3 yields $6 million extra, than the popular and traditional Method 1, in the examples of this chapter.

Therefore, the money tree methods of this chapter can turn the stones and bricks of our house into gold. The intelligent use of debt to grow money trees can produce wealth for us that far exceeds the income of working hard at a job.

This chapter shows that an important money tree method is to "breed" rental properties (Method 2). It can produce a high rate of return with the intelligent use of leverage. The next chapter discusses the importance of leverage in investing.

Chapter 8. Give Me a Lever and I Can Move the Earth

Myth: **Leverage is risky.**

Money Tree: **Grow wealth by maintaining leverage.**

The last chapter included Method 2 with the purchase of rental properties using leverage. After a landlord owns some rental properties for several years, with property value appreciation and paying down the loans, s/he will increase the equity in the properties. Increasing equity means reducing the leverage. This chapter discusses how to maintain leverage for landlords, and how to avoid the decrease of leverage over time. The goal is to maintain a high rate of return to grow wealth.

For example, if the current house price is $500,000 and the landlord owes the bank $200,000, then the landlord has $300,000 equity in that house.

If the landlord has five such rental houses, that means $1.5 million of equity sitting in the houses. If the landlord has ten such houses, that means $3 million of equity. Furthermore, if the landlord has eventually paid off the mortgages of some of the houses, that means even more equity.

I talk with many landlords. Some say: "Yes, I am free! No mortgages!" Some say: "I still have a lot of loans, but after years of paying the mortgages, the equity is increasing nicely." Some say: "I still owe the banks some money, but I have more equity than the loan amount. And the loans will be paid off soon."

Therefore, it is quite common among landlords to have substantial amounts of equity in their rental properties.

However, does it make financial sense to have substantial equity sitting in the properties? How can the equity be used to grow more money for the landlord?

1. Leverage: Give Me a Lever and a Place to Stand, and I Will Move the Earth

The famous Greek mathematician, philosopher and scientist Archimedes used this bold statement to illustrate the power of the lever: "Give me a lever and a place to stand, and I will move the earth."

To illustrate the power of leverage, let's assume that you have $400,000 cash to invest in real estate. In example 1, you buy a rental house at the price of $400,000, and you pay cash with no leverage. Assume that the house appreciates in value at 5% each year. After one year, you have earned in appreciation $400,000 x 5% = $20,000.

In example 2, you use leverage with 20% down payment and 80% loan. With the $400,000 cash as down payment, you buy five houses instead of only one house. After one year, each house appreciates by 5%, or $20,000. With five houses, your value of appreciation = $20,000 x 5 = $100,000. It is 5 times the value of appreciation in example 1, in which leverage was not used.

Your use of leverage has amplified your appreciation fivefold.

This is a simple illustration of the power of leverage. In a more exact calculation, you will need extra money to pay for closing costs, and you will have rental income and mortgage payments. Without getting into too much detail, this simple illustration shows the power of leverage.

What about risk? That is an important topic. Leverage is to be used intelligently with safeguards and risk-control. The investor should "protect the downside, and the upside will take care of itself." The investor should avoid pitfalls and remember: "Tell me where I'm going to die so I will never go there." These safeguards are discussed in my first book *$5 Million in 8 Years: Real Estate Investing on the Side*, and are not repeated here.

2. Pull Cash out of the Equity in Rental Properties to Buy More Properties

My wife and I would like to hold our rental properties for

the long term. This allows the appreciation and principal reduction to continue uninterrupted. In addition, this reduces expenses such as real estate agent commissions and closing costs including transfer taxes every time we buy or sell.

Long term holding means paying down the mortgages and increasing the equity in the properties over time. My wife and I use the equity in our rental properties to continue to grow our wealth.

In the past years, whenever we had a lot of equity in some of our properties, we used cash-out refinances multiple times as well as a line of credit to pull some of the equity out, and used the cash to buy more properties. That reduced the equity in the houses, increased the leverage, increased the rate of return, and resulted in us owning more rental properties.

Similarly, if you start real estate investing, you too can pull the equity out to buy more rental properties. You can do this repeatedly because after several more years, the equity in your properties will grow again due to principal reduction and price appreciation, and you can do cash-out refinances again to buy more properties. For example:

This year, you do cash-out refinancing on house A.

Next year, you do cash-out refinancing on house B.

The following year, you do cash-out refinancing on house C, etc.

This helps spread them out so that when you invest the cash, you are doing annual dollar cost averaging.

By pulling cash out of the equity to buy more rental

properties, the rate of return can be increased significantly. As shown in my first book, the rate of return can be increased by 10% or more when using proper leverage. For example, I increased the rate of return on the invested capital from under 10% to over 25%, via the proper use of leverage (real life deals are demonstrated in my first book *$5 Million in 8 Years*, and are not repeated here).

Even when using a conservative example where you increase your return by just 5%, say, from 15% to 20%, the difference is still quite large after 20 years. For illustrative purposes, assume that your initial investment is $300,000. After 20 years:

At 15% return rate: $300,000 x 1.15**20 = $4.9 million.
At 20% return rate: $300,000 x 1.20**20 = $11.5 million.

Therefore, a few percentage points in annual return can produce a huge difference in the end result. How do we increase the rate of return? By using leverage. Increasing our leverage in an intelligent way can significantly increase our rate of return. Therefore, the money tree method in this chapter can potentially make millions of dollars of additional wealth for you.

3. Pull Cash out of the Equity in the Houses to Buy Stocks

While my wife and I keep our eyes open for more real estate deals, we do not want the money to sit around and do nothing, so we also invest in stocks. My wife and I do not invest in individual stocks. I do not have the talent to beat the Wall Street experts in selecting stocks. I do not want to put in the extra work to research the stocks, with the associated emotional stress. Therefore, I simply put our money into an S&P 500 index fund that charges a low fee of 0.04%. In addition, my 401k is also 100% in the S&P 500, and I look at it only once a year. It is stress-free and "do-nothing". It saves me time and suits my personal preference.

My wife and I borrowed money from the banks and dumped it into an S&P 500 index fund, as described in Chapter 1. This method has produced $283,000 of net profit for us in 2020, and we plan to let this money tree grow for a long time.

The focus here is not in trying to time the market. The point is: In the short term, the S&P 500 goes up and down. No one knows what it will do next week or next month. However, in the long term, it has returned about 10% annually on average from 1965-2020.

In the future, maybe once a year, maybe every couple of years, whenever the equity grows sufficiently in some of our rental properties, my wife and I plan to do cash-out refinances or use a line of credit to borrow more money from the banks and dump it into the S&P 500.

Since we put money into the S&P 500 over multiple years, we are doing some type of "dollar cost averaging". When people say "dollar cost averaging", they usually mean investing a certain amount every two weeks or monthly. Since the "dollar cost averaging" that I describe here is more like once a year, it may be called "annual dollar cost averaging".

The S&P 500 will crash, and it will boom. How do you control this risk? I use two ways to control the risk: (1) Pour money into S&P 500 over multiple years with dollar cost averaging; (2) Hold it for the long term, for example, 15 years.

Based on my collection of data from 2011 to 2019 in my neighborhood, if I own a rental townhouse without leverage, its average annual return is about 7.5% on the invested capital. This includes the cash flow and the house value appreciation.

In contrast, by using leverage, our rental properties have rates of return over 20%, sometimes 40%, as shown in my book *$5 Million in 8 Years: Real Estate Investing on the Side*.

For illustrative purposes, assume that our overall rate of return (a mixture of rental properties and the S&P 500) is an intermediate 15%.

Let's look at the difference with or without leverage. Assume you invest $1 million, and hold the investments for 20 years:

No leverage, having 7.5% annual return: $1 million x 1.075**20 = $4.25 million.

Maintaining leverage, having 15% annual return: $1 million x 1.15**20 = $16.37 million.

The use of leverage grows the wealth by $12 million more than it would be without using leverage.

Maintaining leverage enables real estate property to grow money faster

Important Point. The proper use of leverage can turn our house and rental properties into money trees to grow wealth. This money tree method of making use of our equity and increasing the leverage in the rental properties can earn millions. Furthermore, all I need to do is provide paperwork such as income, assets and tax returns to the loan officer, and then spend an hour to close and sign the documents. After closing, I dump the cash-out money into an S&P 500 index fund. This totals only several hours of my time per year, which can lead to millions of dollars of additional wealth for us and our loved ones to enjoy.

If you feel nervous about cash-out refinances and are afraid of putting the cash into an equity index fund, remember the two keys:

(1) Dollar cost averaging; and

(2) Holding it for the long term.

Also remember what the great boxer Muhammad Ali said: "He who is not courageous enough to take risks will accomplish nothing in life."

Summary. The simple money tree method that I describe in this chapter will help maintain leverage and increase the overall rate of return, with very little additional time and effort. Our wealth will compound much faster this way rather than having a lot of equity sitting in the real estate properties, doing nothing.

This chapter focuses on the use of equity in our rental properties to grow wealth. The next chapter focuses on another important weapon: positive carry.

Chapter 9. Positive Carry

Myth: **Live a debt-free and interest-free life.**

Money Tree: **Positive carry + compounding is a simple method to plant money trees and make millions.**

1. What Is Positive Carry?

Positive carry refers to the method in which the investor borrows money in order to invest it to make a profit on the difference between the interest paid and the interest earned.

In the financial world including Wall Street, many professionals use the positive carry method. They hold two offsetting positions in a particular investment where the cash inflow from one position exceeds the cash outflow from the opposite position. This positive difference is their profit and is called positive carry. For example, they may borrow a currency with a low interest rate while buying another currency that pays high interest, and they pocket the difference.

Positive carry is popular among professional investors,

and there are luxury yachts that are named *Positive Carry*.

Ordinary people like me usually cannot do what Wall Street does, such as playing with international currencies. This chapter describes an unorthodox and innovative method for ordinary people to also benefit from positive carry.

2. My Friend's Positive Carry

Many years ago, I had a friend in China who had high-level connections. He was able to borrow money from a bank at a very low interest rate, and then loan this money out to others at a normal market interest rate, making a difference of about 3%. Although the 3% difference was small, his base amount was big. So, do not look down on the small 3% positive carry. For example, if his base amount was 100 million yuan, 3% means 3 million yuan of passive income each year.

Most of us do not have the connections to make such easy positive carry money. But if you have a good amount of equity in your house and rental properties, you can make positive carry money too. And your positive carry is 6% to 7% in the low interest rate environment of 2020, as shown below.

3. John and Peter

What I personally have been doing, and what you can do too, is this: I borrow money from John at 4% interest. Then I turn around and give the money to Peter, and Peter pays me

10%. I sit at home and do nothing, and get my positive carry of 6% per year.

Furthermore, I re-invest that 6% positive carry, and my wealth grows by compounding over time.

For illustrative purposes, assume that a middle-aged employee, Fred, has been diligently paying his mortgage for many years. His house is now valued at $800,000 and he owes the bank $100,000. This means that he has $700,000 equity in his house.

Using the positive carry method, he can do a cash-out refinance with a bank and borrow, say, $500,000. Since this is his primary residence, he can obtain a relatively low interest rate of about 3% (as of writing this in September 2020). He turns around and dumps that $500,000 into an S&P 500 index fund that returns 10% annually, and he holds it for the long term. His difference (positive carry) is a whopping 7%.

Here is another example. In this case, a landlord owns several rental properties with a total value of $5 million. After years of paying the mortgages, she now owes the bank $1 million in loans. Hence, she has $4 million in equity.

Using the positive carry method, she can do a refinance with lenders to borrow, say, $2 million. With rental properties, her interest rate is higher, say, at 4%. She puts that $2 million in the S&P 500, which returns 10% annually in the long term, and she harvests the positive carry of 6%.

Therefore, if you can borrow $1 million from the banks on the equity in your properties, that yields $60,000/year of earnings for you for doing nothing. If you can borrow $2 million from the banks on the equity in your properties, then you receive $120,000 per year of passive income. Furthermore, this income can go into the compounding magic machine to experience the eighth wonder of the world, as shown in the chart.

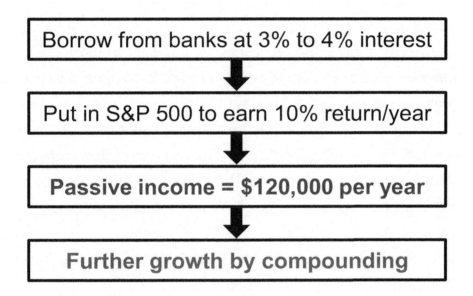

4. Positive Carry + Compounding

Now let's consider the compounding magic. The loan that you owe the bank has a fixed amount; if you borrow $1 million, then it is $1 million. However, when you turn around and put this $1 million into the S&P 500, it will double or triple over the long term. When it doubles after a number of years, then your 10% return from the S&P 500 is calculated based on the $2 million. When it triples to $3 million, then your 10% return is calculated based on the $3 million.

In contrast, your loan from the bank is just $1 million; it does not increase to $2 million or $3 million.

Your investment is compounding, but your loan amount is not compounding. The difference (your investment balance - your loan) will become increasingly large after long-term compounding.

This means that your interest payment to the bank for the loan will become increasingly negligible compared to your profit, when you do this for, say, 15 years.

Hence, as long as my rental properties can break even or produce a small cash flow, the more I can borrow from the banks, the better. Of course, I have safeguards in place to minimize the risk, as described in my first book.[1]

5. Interest-Free Loan to Put into the Long-Term Compounding Magic Machine

Furthermore, since the Federal Reserve has cut interest rates to near 0 (as of writing this in September 2020), it would be highly advantageous if you could lock in an interest rate of, say, 3%. Since the interest payment in real estate is tax-deductible, after the tax benefits, you are only paying an effective interest of about 2%. With the inflation being typically at around 2%, it means that you are effectively paying nearly 0% in "real" interest rate.

Therefore, thanks to the Federal Reserve, it is virtually an interest-free loan.

Think and grow rich. Think about this as a free benefit handed out by the Federal Reserve: Why refuse a free benefit?

Furthermore, think about using this free benefit to plant a free money tree for your family.

As Napoleon Hill said: "Both poverty and riches are the offspring of thought."[2]

It should be noted that when I use the positive carry method to borrow money from the lenders using our houses as collateral and put the cash into the S&P 500, I control my risks. For example, if one borrows money from his house and does day-trading, he could lose it all. What I do is not stock-trading. I don't trade stocks. I know my limits. I know my circle of competence. Furthermore, this is not short term.

I don't do short-term investing. I like real estate with leverage for the high rate of return. However, at some point, my wife and I feel that we have enough rental properties, and don't feel like buying more properties, at least not in 2020. The prices of houses in my neighborhood have increased quite a lot in 2020. It is good news for the houses that we already have, but it dampens my enthusiasm to buy more.

The equity is increasing nicely in our rental properties. Do we let the equity sit in the houses, doing nothing?

That would be wasting a good opportunity to grow wealth for the family. I don't want to waste this opportunity.

That's why I am doing positive carry.

Stage 1. In the past years, my wife and I did cash-out refinances and lines of credit to borrow money from the lenders, and we used the cash to buy more real estate.

Stage 2. Now that we have a good real estate portfolio, we feel like taking a break and not buying more properties in 2020. So, we did cash-out refinances and lines of credit to borrow money from the lenders, and put that cash into the S&P 500.

The positive-carry idea is that we pay low interest to the bank, and the S&P 500 pays us about 10% in the long term (10% average return from 1965-2019). The difference is our positive carry. It is passive, requiring very little time and effort.

If I lock in an interest rate of 3%, then my positive carry is about 7%.

If I lock in an interest rate of 4%, then my positive carry is about 6%.

Furthermore, when invested in the S&P 500, the positive carry is growing more and more wealth by compounding.

We plan to do more cash-out refinances in future years, for example, in 2021, 2022 and 2023, on houses A, B and C, respectively. The cash will be invested in the S&P 500.

Because the money is invested year after year after year, we put the money into the S&P 500 via dollar cost averaging. This could be called yearly dollar cost averaging, instead of monthly.

In the short term, it is risky because the S&P 500 goes

up and down. Its short-term behavior is unpredictable. Therefore, it takes courage to do this.

In the long term, the S&P 500 should revert to its historic average, which returns about 10% per year.

The positive-carry method that I use is easy, simple, passive, and lucrative. However, it requires long-term patience. It is not a way to "get-rich-quick."

It's a money tree that, once I spend a few hours to plant, will continue to grow money year after year, without needing me to spend much time. It is suitable for someone like me who wants a good quality of life and to not have to spend much time to grow wealth.

6. Plant Free Money Trees for Your Family

If you can borrow money from the bank at a real interest rate of almost 0%, why not borrow more money from the bank, and then turn around and plant that money to grow a money tree for your family?

Even if you plant only a small tree, it will grow over the years into a big money tree due to positive carry + compounding magic.

Therefore, think and grow rich. Think through this money tree process. Plant vivid pictures in your mind, then take action.

The lucrative positive-carry opportunity is there in plain sight. However, those who do not think about it will not see it. Opportunity could be screaming in their faces and they wouldn't see it.

The saying "think and grow rich" is true and can be personally experienced and repeated. This chapter invites you to think and imagine your money trees. If the math makes sense to you, then borrow as much money as possible (with safeguards) from John at 3% interest rate, and give it to Peter, who pays you 10% return per year.

The positive carry + the compounding magic will grow your money trees and give you financial freedom, while you spend very little time and effort.

You may read this chapter and say: "Wow, the money tree methods are wonderful. Investing indeed can enable me and my family to reach financial freedom. I want to invest too. But, can I invest anytime? Should I wait for the market to crash first? What if there is a crash in the future? Should I time the market?" Well, the next chapter is for you.

Chapter 10. My Crystal Ball Is in the Repair Shop

Myth: **Predict and time the market to get rich.**

Money Tree: **Keep investing intelligently and persistently for a decade, and you will reach financial freedom.**

1. Investing in Real Estate and the Stock Market

Theodore Roosevelt said: "Every person who invests in well-selected real estate in a growing section of a prosperous community adopts the surest and safest method of becoming independent, for real estate is the basis of wealth."[1]

Indeed, according to Andrew Carnegie: "Ninety percent (90%) of all millionaires become so through owning real estate. More money has been made in real estate than in all industrial investments combined. The wise young man or wage earner of today invests his money in real estate."[2]

My wife and I are ordinary employees. We have had 0 financial inheritance. We raise three kids and pay for their college expenses. We send money to help parents and relatives. We give to our church. We did not save much money in nearly two decades of working hard at our jobs. However, by investing on the side, our net worth increased rapidly, as detailed in my first book *$5 Million in 8 Years*.

We invest in both real estate and the stock market. We want to share our experience with others so that other working families can achieve financial freedom.

Some people read my first book and asked me: "When should I buy a rental house? Has the best time for buying rental houses already passed?"

Some say: "You got lucky in the good old days. We cannot do this anymore."

Some people also discuss with me about investing in the stock market: "The market is so high. Should I wait for a crash, and then invest?"

Some feel regret: "The last decade was a great time to invest in the S&P 500. Why didn't I start doing it in year 2009? Now it seems too expensive and too late."

2. The Past

Regarding the timing of the market, let's say that John Smith read some real estate books and wanted to start to buy rental houses.

He was unlucky. He saved enough down payment and bought his first rental house in 2007 near the peak, right when the once-in-a-life-time housing market crash was about to start.

After his purchase, the market tanked.

In 2008, Fannie Mae and Freddie Mac failed and were bailed out by the government. AIG failed and was bailed out. Lehman Brothers went into bankruptcy.

John Smith was a simple guy; he could not time the market. Neither could I.

However, John Smith was persistent. He stuck to his simple plan: "Save enough money as down payment and buy a house as rental property. Then save more money and buy another house. Then keep repeating this."

In 2009, after two years, he saved enough money as down payment and bought his 2nd rental house.

In 2011, he bought his 3rd rental house.

In 2013, he bought his 4th rental house.

His salary income gradually increased. His cash flow gradually increased. And he could buy a house each year.

In 2014, he bought his 5th rental house.

In 2015, he bought his 6th rental house.

His earlier houses had appreciated in value. In 2016, he did cash-out refinances to pull cash out to buy two houses: his 7th, and 8th.

In 2017, he bought his 9th rental house.

In 2018, he bought his 10th rental houses.

Then he smiled and said: "This is enough. I will stop

buying. I will enjoy life."

The earlier houses that he bought have more cash flow now due to rent increases. His mortgages are being gradually paid down every month. Houses have been appreciating in value. He has gradually established a network of professionals to help him.

His money trees are doing well. He is happy.

Of course, there should be safeguards, as described in my first book *$5 Million in 8 Years: Real Estate Investing on the Side*, to control and minimize the risks.

John Smith lives in a medium-housing-price market. He is satisfied with ten houses: His ten money trees.

If you live in a relatively low-priced housing market, maybe you will acquire 20 houses.

If you live in a relatively expensive housing market, maybe you will buy a house every 3 years. In 10-15 years, you will buy, for example, 7 houses. In an expensive area such as San Francisco, maybe 7 big money trees would be enough, depending on your own situation.

It may take you a decade, or maybe 8 years, or maybe 13 years, depending on your income, cash flow, how many times you do cash-out refinances, as well as your location.

Once you have planted enough money trees, hold them for the long term. Over time, with increasing rent, principal reduction, and property value appreciation, you will secure financial freedom for yourself and your loved ones.

3. The Future

Time flies. Now it was year 2020, and John Smith wanted to share his experience and help others reach financial freedom too.

He started with helping his neighbors. His neighbors on one side were Amanda and her husband Alex (AA). The neighbors on the other side were Bella and Ben (BB). The neighbors across the street were Chelsea and Charlie (CC).

John invited them to his backyard patio to enjoy a bonfire, of course with social distancing and masks. John described his investments to them.

AA said: "Awesome, awesome. We do have quite some cash sitting in the bank earning 0.2% interest. We will do some research and thinking, and will then invest."

BB said: "But, but, the best decade has already ended. You got lucky in the past decade. We have quite a bit of cash in the bank too, but pouring that cash into buying rental houses is risky, because housing prices have already gone up, and the future is so uncertain. Some bad things could happen in the future. The best time for investing has passed."

CC said: "I see. I see. Wow, investing can make such a big difference. Thanks for sharing. You did very well. We will invest too. We do not want to deal with rentals and tenants, so we will invest in the stock market. But, the market is so high now. What should we do?"

John Smith told CC: "You can do it the same way as I

did, with dollar cost averaging. Instead of buying a house every year, you can save money and then put it into an S&P 500 index fund every month. Just be persistent and keep doing it for the long term, such as fifteen years."

4. Predicting the Future and Timing the Market

This old proverb is right: "It's difficult to make predictions, especially with regards to the future."

People who try to time the market usually make less money than those who hold it for the long term. A few people who time the market may make big bucks, but the chance of that is small and similar to the probability of winning the lottery. Some hedge fund managers time the market and win big in one year, and it becomes big news. However, they may time the market again and lose it in subsequent years.

Your friends may tell you about their winning bets, but no one talks about their losing bets. If you were a college student and you got an A+ in an exam, you would talk about it. If you got an F, you would probably not talk about it.

The keywords in investing are "consistent" and "long term." They provide a proven way to financial freedom. These two key words are major challenges facing the market timers.

Indeed: "The stock market is never obvious. It is designed to fool most of the people, most of the time."[3]

If you can truly time the market consistently and do it long term, you would be a big bright star on Wall Street.

In addition, trying to time the market leads to a stressful and anxious life. You may think that the stocks will decline, and you sell them. Then the stocks unexpectedly shoot up. Oops, you have just missed the big surge. Due to the fear of missing out (FOMO), you hurriedly buy them, unfortunately, at or near the top. After you buy them, they drop.

You are competing with professionals who do this for a living with Bloomberg terminals and superfast computers, well-connected managers who have access to much more data than you do, as well as big investors who can move a stock's price.

Indeed, if you invested $1,000 in the market in 1990 and did nothing, it grew to $17,281 by 2019.[4] In contrast, if you tried to time the market and missed out on the ten best-performing months, your $1,000 grew to only $7,000 by 2019.[4] You would have lost more than $10,000, compared to the "lazy" guy who enjoyed a relaxing life and did nothing.

Hindsight is always 20/20. But the future is always uncertain. The future is unknowable. Surprises happen.

The world and the market can change quickly. For example: Black Monday, 9/11, wars, Enron (the Wall Street darling), Lehman Brothers, and Covid-19.

On 8/13/1979, *BusinessWeek* published a famous article entitled: "The Death of Equities: How Inflation Is Destroying the Stock Market." Unfortunately for the forecaster, that was just before the dawn of one of the strongest bull markets of the 1980s and 1990s. From 1982 to 2019, the S&P 500, with dividends reinvested, went up by a whopping 7,000%.

In 2020, the stock market's rapid rise in April and May caught many investors by surprise. They did not expect this strong rally in the doom and gloom of the Covid-19 pandemic. Some experts predicted that this "will end in tears." However, if this scary prediction had convinced you to sell, you would have missed significant gains in the market. Others predicted that it was going to be a long, hot, up-and-down, go-nowhere summer in the stock market. Actually, the S&P 500 index increased from 3056 on June 1, to 3500 on August 30. I do not blame them. These are smart and knowledgeable experts. However, predicting the market's short-term behavior is a losing game.

Therefore, regarding forecasters, there is a saying on Wall Street: "Nobody knows nothing!"

Mr. Buffett said: "Forecasts may tell you a great deal about the forecaster; they tell you nothing about the future."[5] Mr. Buffett basically ignores economic predictions: Don't worry about economic predictions. They just make guesses.[6]

As the joke goes: "If all the market forecasters were laid end to end, they would not reach a conclusion." Even if they did reach a conclusion, it is likely not the correct conclusion.

Some people try to time the market and they may win this time, but lose the next time. The chance of winning may be similar to gambling or flipping a coin.

If you can consistently predict and time the market, you can make a lot of money, and you are among a very small percentage of top investors. Congratulations to you. However, the majority of ordinary people and small investors will not be able to reproduce what you do. This book focuses on money tree methods that are reproducible by ordinary small investors.

For the vast majority of ordinary small investors, myself included, we admit: "My crystal ball is in the repair shop."

5. How to Manage the Risk?

I cannot predict the future, so how do I control and minimize the risks? At the end of 2020, the market is expensive. Where are we right now in the market? Does it feel like 1999?

For me, personally, I don't do these things: (1) I don't invest in individual stocks, (2) I don't do short-term trading, and (3) I don't chase the high fliers.

I do these things: (1) I hold real estate with positive cash flow, (2) I invest in the S&P 500 via dollar cost averaging, and hold it for the long term, and (3) I'm preparing more bullets.

6. Financial Freedom

After the meeting with John Smith, AA did their analyses. They made up their minds: Save the down payment to buy the first rental house, then save and buy the second, then repeat.

They pull the trigger. They buy their first rental house in 2021. They continue to save for the down payment. They buy their second rental in 2023. They buy their 3rd house in 2025.

In 2026, they open a home equity line of credit (HELOC) on their primary residence, and use the money as down payment to buy two rental houses (4th, 5th).

In 2028, they buy their 6th rental. In 2029, with the help of cash-flow accumulation, they buy their 7th and 8th rental houses. In 2030, they do a cash-out refinance on their earlier houses with a lot of equity, and buy two more (9th, 10th).

Then they smile and stop buying. Their rent increases, principals are being paid down, and the houses appreciate over time. With their substantial cash flow and assets, AA have realized their financial freedom.

CC save as much money as they can, and put it in the S&P 500 every month. They do passive investing, hold it for the long term, and ignore the ups and downs.

Twelve years later, in year 2032, when John Smith and his family come back from a month-long vacation in Europe, they get together again in the backyard of John Smith.

AA say to John: "Thank you for your advice 12 years ago. We could never have dreamed that we could achieve so much in a dozen years. We now have financial freedom!"

CC say: "Yes, thank you so much John. We have also achieved our dream of financial freedom!"

BB worry about job security, company downsizing, and having to learn new skills to compete with younger employees. In addition, they are not happy about treatment by their bosses. BB look to the new decade ahead, and say: "It is too late now. We are too old to invest in these risky assets. The future is so uncertain. Bad things could happen."

7. Listen to Those Who Have Done It

The naysayers often say: "This cannot be done now. He got lucky and did it in the good old days. The golden time has already passed. You cannot do it anymore."

Do not listen to the naysayers. Do not listen to those who have not done it. Listen to those who have done it.

If you were going to train yourself to run a marathon, would you take advice on how to run a marathon from those who have never run a marathon themselves? Of course not. You would be listening to those who have actually trained and run marathons themselves.

Every decade, there are some people who invest persistently and reach financial freedom. Every decade, some people take action, pull the trigger, and achieve success.

Every decade, there are others who play it safe. Then after the decade has passed, they look back and regret that they did not start ten years ago. Every decade, the naysayers doubt and criticize and wait, as the decade passes.

Every now and then, you hear about someone who bet on the hot stock and, by a stroke of luck, won big. But that chance is very small. That probability is perhaps similar to that of winning the lottery. When you try to do it yourself, you find that it is very difficult to reproduce the results.

Important Point. The money tree methods of this chapter are reproducible. Some may achieve financial freedom in 8 years; others may achieve it in 10 to 15 years. People who are willing to make a persistent effort will find that the long-term returns and the steady wealth-accumulation strategies in this chapter are reproducible. By being persistent for about a decade, one can indeed achieve financial freedom.

Let's not waste opportunities in the next decade. Do not let anyone tell you that you cannot do it. It is your life. Block out the noise. Listen to your heart. Be courageous. Be bold. Be tough. Be resilient. Be optimistic.

I hope that this chapter will help you to analyze and then have the courage to pull the trigger to get started. We have only one life on this earth. Our time is limited. Someday not too long from now, we will have to leave. How many good opportunities and good fights will we have in our lifetime? When we are old, sitting in an armchair and looking back, wouldn't it be regrettable if we did not try?

Chapter 11. Do You Have Cash Flow or Alligators?

Myth: They both have $3 million, so they are the same.

Money Tree: Build up cash flow. Avoid alligators.

The previous chapter focuses on persistently investing for a decade to reach financial freedom. Ordinary people can learn to use the money tree methods and continue for a decade, and they will achieve financial security. However, some people misunderstand it, and they mix up financial freedom with net worth. For example, Bob and Kelly both have a net worth of $3 million. Are they the same? Do they both have financial freedom? This important topic is discussed in this chapter.

In April 2020, a friend of mine was laid off by his company. That same month, another friend lost his job. He was my classmate and one of the top three students in our class. In August, I learned that another friend had lost his job. All three were engineers. One was 56 years old, and the other two were in their early 50s. One of them moved into a bigger house about five years ago. One family moved into a bigger house last year. They had kids who were either in college or were about to start college next year. All three of them were hard-working and excellent people. None had rental properties or passive cash flow. They were looking for jobs and were under a lot of stress.

I hope this chapter will help people pay attention to passive cash flow.

1. House-Rich Does Not Mean Financial Freedom

A couple of months ago, while talking about real estate in a group chat, someone posted pictures of a beautiful house on the market for sale in California. The price was $9 million. Then, another friend in the group chat posted another house on the market in an expensive neighborhood near Washington DC, and the asking price was $5 million.

These pictures reminded me of a news report that I read years ago. An upper level manager bought a house for his family with his wife and two kids that cost more than $25 million. As you would imagine, the monthly mortgage payment was huge. He had a big salary that could afford the mortgage payments, but after paying all the living expenses, there was little money left. When the recession hit and layoffs started, he became increasingly anxious. His boss saw his anxiety, had a talk with him and told him that there's nothing he needed to worry about. However, he kept worrying about what would happen if he lost his job and couldn't pay the mortgage. Eventually, he committed suicide. A sad story.

I wonder what would have happened if, instead of purchasing the $25 million house, he had bought a $5 million house for the family. Then he invested the rest of his money in rental houses or apartment buildings that generated positive cash flow. The cash flow would have provided for his family and given him peace of mind. He would have had multiple money trees that grew money for him, instead of one big house that he had to feed big money into every month.

2. George and Linda

To illustrate the importance of cash flow, let's consider two people, George and Linda.

George lives in an expensive neighborhood and he has $3 million net assets. His assets are mostly in his big primary residence and his retirement plan. He has no passive cash flow, so he has to rely on his paychecks from his employment to feed money into his house every month.

Linda also has $3 million in net assets. She likes real estate. Her assets are in rental houses, in addition to her home. Her rentals spit out about $100,000 net positive cash flow each year. She likes her job and is still working, but this passive cash flow can enable her to quit her job and travel the world, if she wants to. She has financial freedom, which provides her with more choices. As Robert Kiyosaki said:[1]

"Financial independence is about having more choices."

It is not just the net worth that is important. The cash flow is key. George and Linda have the same $3 million net asset value. But Linda has passive cash flow. George does not.

3. Money Tree versus Alligator

Therefore, an important question is: How much passive cash flow do I have? If my asset spits out cash every month, then I have a money tree.

People say: "Money does not grow on trees." However, if you have rental properties with positive cash flow, they are like money trees that grow money for you. They are like your peach trees that grow peaches for you once a year, or your apple trees that grow apples for you once a year - except that your rental properties grow money for you every month.

In contrast, if you have to feed money into your big house every month, then you have an "alligator" that eats cash.

During an economic recession or a company-downsizing, some people lose their jobs. Those who have "alligators" that require the feeding of money every month, such as a big mortgage and property taxes, may lose their houses. They get financially "eaten" by the "alligator".

For example, about 10 million Americans lost their homes during the financial crisis of 2008.

Therefore, it is important to know that Linda has a money

tree. In contrast, George has an "alligator."

As some people say: "Do not let my big house and boat fool you; I am broke."

4. Use "Risk" to Kill Risk

Some friends who invest in real estate told George in the past years about real estate investing. But George said: "Real estate investing is risky. I do not want the stress."

This year, George reaches 50 years of age. Now, the company is downsizing. Rumor has it that 10% of the workforce will be let go. Often, employees age 50 or older are let go. By the time they have reached 50, their salaries have increased over the years. They are more expensive than those with fresh, cutting-edge knowledge who are in their twenties.

George needs his paychecks to feed money into his house. Now he is very worried that he will be let go by the company. That would mean that he would not have money to feed into his house. Then he would lose his house. He would have to sell his big house and buy a small house. Or, he may have to move to another part of the country wherever another company may offer him a job. Either way is quite a traumatic experience for the family, and a stressful situation.

Now, for George and Linda, guess who is more stressed out, and whose choice is more risky?

As Suze Orman said: "A big part of financial freedom is having your heart and mind free from worry about the what-ifs of life."[2]

Real estate investing seems risky. However, as demonstrated in my first book *$5 Million in 8 Years*,[3] real estate actually reduces and minimizes financial risk. By acquiring properties wisely, building a team, negotiating good deals, and expanding through an intelligent use of leverage, an ordinary person like me can grow money trees for my family.

Real estate investing can neutralize the risk of losing a job, or of other unexpected events in life. By growing money trees, you provide financial security to your family.

Once you have substantial cash flow, you have more choices. You can choose to work. You can choose to fire your boss if your boss is nasty. You can choose a less stressful and more pleasant job. You can choose to work part-time, or quit altogether. You can travel the world. You can pursue your passion and your hobby. You have the ability to give and help others. You have more freedom.

Medicine is bitter, but it yields healing and good health. Real estate investing seems risky, but it actually lowers risk and yields good financial health for you and your loved ones.

5. Summary

George and Linda have the same amount of $3 million assets. The QUANTITY is the same. But the QUALITY is different.

Linda's asset is a money tree. George's is an alligator.

If your rental property produces cash every month, it is a money tree.

If the property requires the feeding of cash, it is an "alligator".

Photo courtesy of my friend Dr. John C.

Furthermore, besides the primary residence, some people have a beach house or a vacation home in a mountain that they have a mortgage on. Some have a boat that they bought with borrowed money. Some have loans on their luxury cars. They have to feed money into these possessions every month; hence, these possessions are alligators.

Therefore, we need to pay attention not only to the quantity of the asset, such as:

"How much money does he have? How many houses and cars does he have?"

More importantly, we should pay attention to the quality and the nature of the asset and ask:

"Does the asset spit out cash every month?"

"How much passive cash flow does it produce?"

"Does the asset eat cash?"

"Is the asset an alligator or a money tree?"

I hope this chapter helps you to more vividly establish the money tree concept, and take action to build up your passive cash flow.

Our purpose for investing is to achieve financial freedom, be able to help others, improve the quality of life, and pursue happiness. Wouldn't it be a wonderful thing if investing could enable us to retire early? Therefore, the next chapter will discuss how to retire early.

Chapter 12. Retire in Your 40s?

Myth: Can ordinary working-class people achieve financial freedom and retire in their 40s? No way!

Money Tree: Can ordinary people achieve early retirement and financial freedom? Yes we can!

"Congratulations on your retirement! Enjoy your never-ending weekend!"

My daughter Sweetie and her husband Moutai came over for dinner on a Saturday. She excitedly announced: "Daddy and Mommy, I want to retire early so that I can travel the world. I also want to do volunteer work."

Then she hesitated: "But I don't want to sacrifice my lifestyle just for the sake of retiring early. I want to have enough money to retire on." Then she looked at me and pleaded: "Dad, you are the expert. Can I do that?"

I smiled at her: "Let me think about a plan."

After a few minutes, I asked her: "You have two options. (1) Do you want to invest in rental properties and be quite wealthy and retire early? (2) Do you want to use a simple and do-nothing method, and retire early with a comfortable life style? The real estate method will accumulate millions more money than the do-nothing method, but the do-nothing method can also provide a comfortable retirement in your 40s."

Sweetie said: "We are not ready to deal with rental properties yet. The do-nothing option sounds attractive! Let's choose the do-nothing way."

I said: "I will put together a do-nothing plan. If you are willing to follow it, yes, you can retire in your 40s. Deal?"

She exclaimed happily: "Deal!"

I spent a few hours the next day, and emailed her a PDF file with the following plan.

Retire in Your 40s via a "Do-Nothing" Investing Method

Hi Sweetie:

Millions of hard-working employees earnestly look forward to retirement: "When every day is Saturday!" But they also worry about money in retirement: "I'm now as free as the breeze. But my income is also as light as the breeze."

Here, I will describe a money tree method that can support your early retirement comfortably, while you do virtually nothing. The "do-nothing" method involves putting money into the S&P 500 periodically, and then forgetting about it. You just look at it when you record your wealth at the end of each year.

In the past two decades, besides investing in real estate,

all my other money has been invested in the S&P 500. It is truly "do-nothing", and I look at it only once a year.

In the past 70 years, the S&P 500 has returned an average of approximately 10% per year.

In order to achieve financial freedom and retire in your 40s, you will need to make an effort to save and invest. I think that you can save 20% of your salary. Your current salary in year 2020 is $70,000. Someone else who makes 80% of your salary ($56,000) is also able to live a reasonably good life.

You work for a big company with a stable job. Based on what you have told me about your company, you expect to get an annually salary increase of around 3-4%. In addition, every several years, you expect to receive a promotion with additional increases in salary. Therefore, it is reasonable to assume that on average, your annual increase in salary will be around 4%.

In the first year of this investing plan, 2020, you are 25 years old. You invest 20% of your salary into the S&P 500. Your company matches 6% for your 401k, which is also put into the S&P 500. Therefore, the total is 26% of your salary.

Year 1, your S&P 500 has: $70,000 x 26% = $18,200.

In year 2, the $18,200 from year 1 grows by 10% to $20,020. In year 2, your salary is increased by 4% to $72,800. And 26% of your salary (= $18,928) goes into the S&P 500.

Therefore, in year 2, your S&P 500 will have a total of: $20,020 (growth from last year) + $18,928 (newly invested amount this year) = $38,948.

In the same way, the subsequent years are calculated,

127

as listed in the Table.

Year	Age	Salary $	Invested $ Amount/Year	S&P 500 Total $
1	25	70,000	18,200	18,200
2	26	72,800	18,928	38,948
3	27	75,712	19,685	62,528
4	28	78,740	20,472	89,253
5	29	81,890	21,291	119,469
6	30	85,166	22,143	153,559
7	31	88,572	23,029	191,944
8	32	92,115	23,950	235,088
9	33	95,800	24,908	283,505
10	34	99,632	25,904	337,759
11	35	103,617	26,940	398,475
12	36	107,762	28,018	466,341
13	37	112,072	29,139	542,114
14	38	116,555	30,304	626,629
15	39	121,217	31,516	720,808
16	40	126,066	32,777	825,666
17	41	131,109	34,088	942,321
18	42	136,353	35,452	1,072,005
19	43	141,807	36,870	1,216,075
20	44	147,479	38,345	1,376,028
21	45	153,378	39,878	1,553,509

By year # 21, when you are 45 years old, you would have reached a total amount of $1,553,509 in your S&P 500. Since the average return of the S&P 500 is about 10% per year, it will spit out $155,351 in annual return, which matches your job's salary for that year. This means that you are getting the same "salary" from your S&P 500 profit, without having to work.

Since the 10% annual return from your S&P 500 investment = your salary, it provides the same amount of income for you, without you having to work. You quit your job, and still receive the same amount of income. This is called passive income. Your money is working for you, so that you do not have to work for money.

You could think of the $1,553,509 in the S&P 500 as a money tree. It grows $155,351 of annual profit for you. You may be in Europe vacationing, or in Asia visiting relatives, or volunteering at a church, and your money tree will keep growing money for you. You have reached your financial freedom.

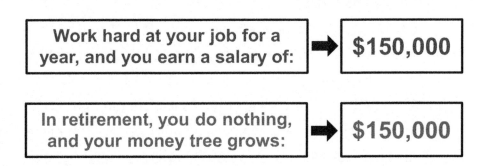

So, your money works for you; hence, you do not have to work for money. Quoting Manoj Arora:

"Stay in your bed as long as you want. Your money just left for work!"[1]

Furthermore, once you have this money tree, it will grow money for you indefinitely. It will continue to grow money for you, even if you live another 100 years in your retirement.

Or, you could also think of the $1,553,509 in your S&P 500 as a printing machine. It legally prints $155,351 of money for you annually.

With your money tree, you have avoided this situation: "Retirement: No deadlines, no tensions, no anxieties, no stress, no money!"

In addition, please note the following six points.

First, since you started working at age 22, you already have some money invested in the S&P 500. The table that I put together for you only counts your new money starting from 2020 when you are 25 years old, without including your investments prior to age 25. Therefore, the aforementioned table is a conservative estimate.

Second, prior to age 45, you put 20% of your salary away into the S&P 500, and use only 80% of your salary. Therefore, when you retire, you can continue to use only 80% of the $155,351, and leave the other 20% invested in the S&P 500. This will further grow and increase your wealth; therefore, the table is a conservative estimate. This will also afford you an additional 2% in passive income each year to account for inflation. In addition, the S&P 500 will go up and down, but since you will hold it for decades, its long-term average annual return is about 10%. No matter if it is up or down, you can just sell a prescribed amount to enjoy your retirement.

Third, while I am not a tax expert and you need to consult with an accountant, the long-term profit from the S&P 500 has a lower tax rate than your salary. This means tax savings, compared to working at a job. This means that, to match your pre-retirement income and lifestyle, you may not need to use all 80% of the $155,351 from your S&P 500, thus leaving even more money invested in the S&P 500 to continue to grow for you.

These three points mean that the aforementioned table is a conservative estimate.

Fourth, to be even more conservative, you may choose to work for a few more years before you retire. For example, if you retire at age 47, instead of 45, it would further increase the total amount in your S&P 500.

Fifth, this is a simple estimate and not an exact calculation. For example, you will most likely make the investment every month instead of once a year. You will invest 6% of your own money into your 401k together with the company's 6% match. For the other 14% of your own money, you can invest into a regular S&P 500 mutual fund, which you can sell some of it annually and use the money before you reach age 59.5. Once you reach age 59.5, then you can also start to sell and use your 401k money.

Sixth, based on your company, you are expected to receive bonuses from time to time, which are not included in this conservative estimate. You may spend your bonuses to indulge yourself, or put it in your S&P 500 for further growth.

You are welcome to share this PDF file with your friends. Since I have laid out the year-by-year table, it will help them do their own calculations. Their salaries are different. Maybe they want to invest 15% of their salary, or 30% of their salary. By following this table, they can set a goal on when to retire and how big their money tree will be, based on their own salaries and personal situations. This will give them the inspiration and encouragement to save and invest persistently to grow their money tree and be able to retire early and comfortably.

Important Point. With persistence in investing (in this example, into a low-fee S&P 500 index fund which beats most mutual funds), even ordinary people with ordinary income can retire comfortably in their 40s. Furthermore, the money tree will grow money each year and continue forever.

This will help you and your friends to reach financial freedom using a simple, "do-nothing" method.

Follow this plan, and you will be able to retire early and comfortably. Your money will continue to work for you indefinitely long into the future, so that you will never have to work for money again.

Love you,
Dad

Using a "do-nothing" money tree method, ordinary people can achieve financial freedom and retire early.

This chapter debunks the myth that ordinary people with ordinary income cannot retire comfortably in their 40s.

This chapter uses my daughter Sweetie as an example. The next chapter generalizes the concept and shows that ordinary people across a wide spectrum, from low income to high income, can achieve early retirement and financial freedom using the money tree methods.

Chapter 13. It's Not the Strongest, Nor the Fastest, But the Most Persistent, Who Will Succeed

Myth: **Whether you can achieve financial freedom depends on your salary level.**

Money Tree: **A decade of persistence leads to life-long financial independence.**

Ordinary people can invest in the stock market and/or real estate to achieve financial freedom, and retire early as millionaires. The previous chapter uses the S&P 500 investment as an example to achieve early retirement. This chapter uses real estate as another example to achieve early retirement.

Whether one uses real estate or the stock market, the key to achieving early retirement and financial freedom is: Persistence.

Indeed, as former Unites States Senator and basketball player Mr. Bill Bradley said: "Ambition is the path to success. Persistence is the vehicle they arrive in."[1]

1. Modest-Income People Invest to Reach Financial Freedom

In my first book *$5 Million in 8 Years: Real Estate Investing on the Side*, I described a schoolteacher who bought 26 rental properties in 20 years, and then retired in her 40s to travel the world. Her salary was modest, but she saved diligently for the down payment to buy her first rental house. Then she saved to buy the second rental house. And she kept going.

After several years, rent increased, giving her significant cash flow to speed up her purchasing of rental houses. After a few more years, with increasing equity in her houses, she did cash-out refinances to pull cash out to buy more properties.

More rental houses produced more cash flow, and more cash flow enabled her to buy more rentals. They fed on each other. This formed a powerful virtuous cycle for her, enabling her to accumulate 26 rental properties in 20 years and retire in her 40s. The key to her success was not her modest salary. The key was persisting long enough to create a virtuous cycle.

And she got there by persisting for 20 years.

Such experiences are actually reproducible. Recently, Mr. Robert Exley reported that a young couple, both schoolteachers with three kids and with modest salaries, invested in rental houses and retired at the age of 29.[2] They graduated from college at the age of 22, and started working as schoolteachers. They reached financial freedom not by inheritance or winning lotteries, but by persistently saving and buying rental properties. As of 2020, the young couple owned 19 rental properties. The cash flow provided for their living expenses, vacations and traveling the world. In addition, the husband volunteers at Habitat for Humanity, and the wife pursues her passion of writing novels.

It is said that "It's not the strongest, nor the fastest, but the most adaptable, who survive and do well." Similarly, it's not necessarily those with the highest IQ, nor those with the highest degrees, but those who are the most persistent in investing, who achieve financial freedom.

Benjamin Franklin predicted the aforementioned successes when he said: "Energy and persistence conquers all things."

2. Low-Income People Invest to Reach Financial Freedom

The following is also a true story, told to me years ago by my former real estate agent, Lilly, who knew a lady named Jenny. Lilly spoke with a tone of admiration about Jenny. Jenny was from humble beginnings and worked at 7-Eleven and a second job at a restaurant. One day, she surprised everyone when she bought a house at a price of over $200,000, which she paid with cash. Yes, she worked really hard, but her total income was a meager $30,000 a year. How did she buy the house with cash?

This was how Jenny did it. She lived in a rented basement room, kept her living expenses to a bare minimum, saved as much as she could every month and invested in the stock market monthly. After about eight years of saving and investing diligently, she bought that house. Because at that time no lender would give her any loans, she sold her stocks and bought the house with cash.

She moved into the house, used one room for herself, and rented out the other rooms to accumulate more cash. After a couple of years, due to her steady (although low) salary, excellent credit history and increasing rental income, a lender approved her home equity line of credit (HELOC) using her house as collateral. She took the HELOC money, paid cash to buy her second house and rented it out.

After six months, she used the second house as collateral and the leases as proof of income, using rent plus salary as her total income justification, to do a cash-out refinance on her second house. She used that cash, plus her savings, to pay cash for her third house, and then rented it out. Over the years, the values of her houses increased, allowing her to do cash-out refinances. She was persistent and kept repeating these steps. Eventually, she owned a dozen houses with about $2 million of equity in them, plus $80,000 in cash flow per year. Then she retired.

The values of Jenny's houses continued to increase with time, her rental income increased every year, and the loans were being paid down. Her persistence enabled her to achieve financial freedom from humble beginnings.

Indeed, as Calvin Coolidge, the 30th United States President, said: "Nothing in this world can take the place of persistence. Nothing is more common than unsuccessful men with talent. Persistence and determination alone are omnipotent."[3]

3. High-Income People Invest to Reach Financial Freedom

There is no guarantee that high-income people have financial freedom. "High income" and "financial freedom" are two different things. There are plenty of people with good salaries who live paycheck to paycheck. They sink their salary income into the big mortgage payment of a luxurious house, fancy cars and a vacation home. However, they have no "money trees" and no passive income. As a result, they are only a few missed paychecks away from exposing their financial fragility. Layoffs due to economic recession or company-restructuring could lead to their financial ruin.

In contrast, I recently interacted with a gentleman named Tim on social media. Tim and his wife both work in the tech industry in California. They are both relatively high earners. Lenders like their salaries and are willing to give them loans. Using savings from their high salaries plus loans from the banks, they bought 20 houses as rental properties in California over the past decade. Tim said that their loan-to-value (LTV) ratio was about 70%. Some of their houses initially had negative cash flow due to the high prices of houses in California, and they used their good salaries to feed into these houses. However, their cash flow started to pick up as rent increased over time. Tim and his wife plan to hold these rental houses for another 5-10 years, then retire and enjoy their financial freedom.

Therefore, low income, modest income and high income people can all achieve financial freedom through investing. The key is "persistence." Keep doing it for a decade, maybe 8 years for some, maybe 15 years for others. Do not give up after 2 years. Do not give up after 4 years. Time and again, example after example, ordinary people with ordinary salaries can achieve financial freedom by investing in real estate persistently for a decade.

Some may say: "These examples are all great. But they happened in the good old days. The golden time for investing has passed. You cannot do this anymore."

I would suggest that you memorize what the legendary Sir John Templeton said: "The four most dangerous words in investing are: 'This time it's different.'"[4]

His original meaning was that some people believe that

while the past bubbles have all burst, the current bubble will be an exception. However, these four words could also be used to describe that, by thinking that this time it's different and there are no more golden opportunities, people miss another decade to make millions to secure their financial freedom. It is important to remember that, for those who are persistent in investing, every decade can be a successful decade. Every decade provides good opportunities and exciting deals for the intelligent small investor.

As we have seen in previous chapters, on the road to financial freedom via investing, a highly important parameter is the rate of return. That is the focus of the next chapter.

Chapter 14. The Return Is the King

Myth: **Cash is king.**

Money Tree: **The rate of return is king.**

The famous "The Lord of the Rings" has this title: "The Return of the King." In investing, I like to say: "The Return Is the King."

1. Focus on the Rate of Return

In William Shakespeare's play, Hamlet, Act 3, Scene 1, Prince Hamlet famously asked: "To be, or not to be?"

In real estate investing, people ask another important question: "To buy, or not to buy?"

The answer depends on the rate of return. A great rate of return is the king. For me, personally, if the rate of return is good and the deal meets my safeguards, I would like to buy. If the return is poor, I walk away.

People often say: "Cash is king." However, that is a myth. If you keep your wealth in cash, it depreciates by about 2% every year due to inflation. For example, if you keep $1 million in cash, you lose $20,000 every year. It is like a block of ice that is slowly melting in the sun, becoming smaller and smaller as time passes.

"Why did he put his money in the freezer? He wanted cold, hard cash." He will preserve his cash this way, but it will not grow. It will depreciate over time.

If I want to grow my wealth and achieve financial freedom, my cash needs to be invested to achieve a good rate of return. Real estate investing has been proven to yield an excellent rate of return for ordinary people.

Some people have asked me: "When is a good time to buy real estate? Has the good time already passed?"

"Should I buy rental houses now? Or, is it too late?"

"Is a crash coming soon? Should I wait?"

"This rental house has only a small cash flow. It is not worth to buy it, right?"

All real estate is local. This chapter shows illustrations using information from my location. However, you can input the numbers from your own location and perform the same estimate as described below, to see what kind of rate of return you will get. That will tell you whether or not you should buy.

Therefore, to answer the question "To buy or not to buy", an important consideration is the rate of return. If the rate of return is good, then it is likely a buy. If the rate of return is too low, then it is not a buy. A small investor should use the rate of return in the decision-making on whether or not to buy a specific rental property, instead of trying to time the market and waiting for a crash.

If, indeed, the market is over-heated and a crash maybe coming, it will be reflected in the price of the house, and you would be over-paying for the house. This will result in a poor rate of return, which serves as a warning sign for you to walk away. Therefore, the rate of return serves as an important safeguard.

For me, personally, if the estimated annual rate of return is around 12%, it is a weak buy. If it is above 15%, it is a buy. If it is above 20%, it is a strong buy.

This is because my alternative is investing in the passive, "do-nothing", S&P 500 index fund, and get a long-term 10% annual return. Therefore, to invest in real estate that involves tenants and repairs, the return must be meaningfully higher than that of the S&P 500.

Therefore, I focus on the rate of return as well as the aforementioned safeguards. The rate of return is where the rubber meets the road. The rate of return is what determines how quickly or slowly my wealth grows.

2. An Example in My Neighborhood

I looked at townhouses in my neighborhood and did the

following estimate, as of November 2020.

A typical three-story townhouse in my neighborhood could be purchased at about $360,000. For a 30 year-fixed mortgage, the interest rate was about 3% for primary residence. For rental property, assume the interest rate was 3.5%. Assume a 20% down payment with 80% loan.

The money that I would throw into this house: Down payment = 20% x $360,000 = $72,000. The closing cost is about $13,000. Total invested capital = $85,000.

The mortgage = 80% x $360,000 = $288,000. At 3.5% interest fixed for 30 years, the monthly principal + interest payment (PI) = $1,293.

The interest part is ($288,000 x 0.035)/12 = $840/month. Hence, the principal reduction is $1,293 - $840 = $453. The principal is basically money that is paid into my own pocket because it reduces the loan amount that I owe the bank. This is a simple estimate. For an exact calculation, please consult a loan officer.

The property tax is about $5,000 annually (or $417/month). The insurance is about $480 annually ($40/month). The home owner's association due is $110 monthly. The estimated repair costs are about $1,000 annually (or $83/month). My neighborhood has relatively new houses with less repair costs.

To find a tenant, my agent charges $1,600, and the average tenant has stayed for about three years in my rental properties. Therefore, the agent fee for finding the tenant and signing the lease is about $1,600/36 = $45/month.

For such a townhouse, the current rent is about $2,150/month. You can probably get $2,200/month, but I usually keep the rent at $50 to $100 below the market. A slightly lower rent attracts more applicants so that I can choose a better tenant, and it reduces the vacancy. The vacancy in my rentals has been less than one month per three years on average, which is $2,150/36 = $60/month on average.

My neighborhood has the best schools in the county, with a relatively high demand from tenants. The three main advantages of buying rental houses in a very good school area are: (1) Housing value appreciation is relatively higher than neighboring locations with mediocre schools; (2) there is a high demand from tenants and hence less vacancy; and (3) the tenants are of relatively higher incomes.

Therefore, based on the aforementioned numbers, the net cash flow = $2,150 - $1,293 - $417 - $40 - $110 - $83 - $45 - $60 = $102/month.

You may think that this cash flow is so small that it is not worth it. However, as you will see below, even if this is 0 (breakeven), the deal may still be lucrative and worth pursuing.

The housing value appreciation in my neighborhood has been 3-4% annually. Assume it is 3.5%. $360,000 x 0.035 = $12,600 in the first 12 months.

Now the important parameter:

Rate of return in the first 12 months = (Cash flow + principal reduction + house value appreciation)/money I throw into this house = ($102x12 + $453x12 + $12,600)/$85,000 = ($1,221 + $5,439 + $12,600)/85,000 = $19,260/$85,000 = 22.7%.

This is a simple estimate. Different investors may use different methods to do the estimate. Some use sophisticated Excel files to do their calculations. The advantage of this simple calculation is that you can replicate it on the back of an envelope when you are looking at a house to buy. Furthermore, it is not necessary to be too exact on such an estimate, for three reasons. (1) I am not looking for an exact number. I just want to see if it meets my 15% criterion or the 20% criterion. (2) These numbers will change over time, because the principal part will grow over time, and the interest part will decrease over time as you owe the bank less and less money. (3) You may do a cash-out refinance after a few years which will change the rate of return. Therefore, there is no need for an exact number. The aforementioned numbers are only for the initial estimate of the rate of return, in order to determine whether it is worth buying or not.

The 22.7% rate of return easily beats the S&P 500's long term average return of 10% per year. It also beats Mr. Warren Buffett's average annual return of 14% in the past quarter century (1994-2019).[1]

3. Is It Worth Buying if There Is No Cash Flow?

Now, let's assume that somehow the repair costs increase and the vacancy increases, and the net cash flow of $102/month disappears. Now, the cash flow = 0.

Rate of return in the first 12 months = (0 + $5,439 + $12,600)/$85,000 = 21.2%.

It still far exceeds the 10% annual return for the S&P 500 and the 14% annual return for Mr. Buffett (1994 - 2019).[1]

Therefore, even if the house has no cash flow, it is not a deal breaker. It may very well still be worth investing.

Certainly, you should look at other factors too. For example, the appreciation rate should be the long-term historic average, not just for the last couple of years. If your area has experienced fast appreciation in the last couple of years, you should not use that fast appreciation rate in your calculation, and expect that the fast growth rate will continue into future years. I would be extremely cautious if the last few years have gone up too fast, because eventually it will drop or slow down and revert to the long-term average. It is also important to do some research to see if people are leaving your area or moving into your area, if the population is growing or declining, if companies are moving in or leaving, whether the area is thriving or decaying, etc.

These and other safeguards, including understanding

the local market, what and when and how to buy, effective negotiation skills to get the lowest possible price, are discussed in details with real life examples in my book *$5 Million in 8 Years: Real Estate Investing on the Side*,[2] and are not repeated here.

4. Is It Worth Buying if There Is Negative Cash Flow?

Now, let's assume an even worse scenario, in which the cash flow is negative: -$100/month. It means that, every month, you have to put $100 into the rental house to cover the expenses. Is such a house worth buying?

Rate of return in the first 12 months = (-$100x12 months + $5,439 + $12,600)/$85,000 = 19.8%.

Even with a negative cash flow, the rate of return still far exceeds the 10% annual return for the S&P 500 and the 14% annual return for Mr. Buffett (1994 - 2019).[1] This is because there is good principal reduction and housing value appreciation to contribute to the rate of return.

Therefore, even if the house has negative cash flow, it may still be worth buying.

Note: With rental houses that have negative cash flow, you have to be careful that you have enough cash to feed into the house. You need to sustain it for a sufficiently long time, say, for a couple of years, until rents have increased to achieve breakeven. For example, if you have a stable job with a good income, then you may be able to afford to own a few rental houses with a small negative cash flow. However, if you rely on cash flow to supplement your income, then negative cash flow rentals are not suitable for you.

5. Three Factors: (1) Cash Flow, (2) Principal Reduction, (3) Appreciation

I have a colleague who grew up in a small town in America. He earned his PhD degree and now works in a big city. Every year, he goes back to visit his parents in that small town. He told me that all the young people he grew up with have left. The companies are gone. There are no job opportunities there. It is a sad situation. You can buy an inexpensive house there and rent it to those who cannot afford to buy a house, and get good cash flow. But the place may continue to deteriorate, and you may have little appreciation in the house value. Your house value may even decrease when you try to sell it in the future.

Therefore, do not look at cash flow alone when you make your decision. You have to look at all three parameters: (1) cash flow, (2) principal reduction, and (3) appreciation.

Among other factors, the monthly rental income and expenses will affect # (1), the interest rate will affect # (2), and the quality of the location and your negotiation skills will affect # (3).

If the cash flow is good, but the appreciation is poor or even negative, then it likely is not a good deal. Therefore, do not focus on cash flow alone.

Furthermore, if the house value appreciation is poor or even negative, it could be due to that people and jobs are leaving, a relatively high crime rate, mediocre schools, contamination in soil and water, hash weather, poor transportation, etc. Therefore, house value appreciation is a key parameter that tells you a lot of important information.

Important Point. You should use all three parameters when you determine if a rental house is worth buying: (1) cash flow, (2) principal reduction, and (3) appreciation. You should look at all three. Do not let a single factor, such as cash flow, to determine your decision, because that can lead to a wrong decision which can cost you.

The rate of return = (cash flow + principal reduction + house value appreciation)/money I throw into this house.

The King: A great rate of return is the king in our investment.

6. The 1% Ratio

To answer the question "To buy or not to buy", some people use the ratio of rent to house value, to determine whether a rental house is worth buying or not. For example, in one definition, if a house can be purchased with $200,000, and can rent for $2,000/month, then the ratio of rent to house value = 1%.

The 1% is an excellent ratio. Many houses that I have seen have a ratio of around 0.7%. And they can yield over 20% in annual return, with the use of leverage. Therefore, if you can buy a rental house that has a 1% ratio, congratulations. If you cannot, that does not mean that you should not invest. Often, a ratio of around 0.7% still yields an excellent rate of return.

Therefore, make sure that you perform the aforementioned estimate using all three parameters, and do not just rely on a single parameter such as the ratio of rent/house value. The following are four illustrations.

Case 1. Assume that John lives in an area where the ratio of rent to house value is only 0.6%. However, his area has a low property tax rate of 0.7%. In addition, at the time of his purchase, he locks in an interest rate of 3% for a 30-year fixed mortgage. As a result, he enjoys a good rate of return on his real estate investment.

Case 2. Jack lives in an area where the ratio of rent to house value is 1%, which is excellent. However, his property tax rate is 2.4%, and at the time of his purchase, the interest rate is 6%. (In the 1990s when my wife and I bought our first house, our interest rate was over 7%). These factors will compromise Jack's rate of return on his rental house. Hence, the 1% ratio does not guarantee a good rate of return.

Case 3. Peter lives in a neighborhood where he can buy rental houses at a rent to house value ratio of 1%, which is excellent. However, there is an exodus of people. Companies and jobs are leaving. Schools are declining. He'd better not invest there, even if the rent to house value ratio is 1%.

Case 4. James is looking to buy rental houses in an old neighborhood. The rent to house value ratio is 1%, which is awesome. However, the houses are 60 years old. They will need a lot of ongoing repairs and maintenance costs which will eat into his return. Furthermore, old houses with old designs such as lower ceilings and smaller windows, along with the need for more repairs, may experience slow appreciation when you try to sell the house in the future. In addition, old houses are more time-intensive for a landlord even if you use contractors to do the repair work. If you are a busy professional doing real estate investing on the side, such old houses may not be suitable for you.

Therefore, as intelligent small real estate investors, we should focus on the rate of return, not the 1% ratio.

As Nobel Laureate Prof. Robert J. Shiller said:

"The ability to focus attention on important things is a defining characteristic of intelligence."[3]

Here, the important thing that we should focus on is the rate of return. Do not get distracted by cash flow alone, or the 1% ratio.

7. Summary

(1) The rate of return = (cash flow + principal reduction + house

value appreciation)/your invested capital into the house.

(2) The rate of return is king.

(3) Focus on the rate of return which is calculated by using all three parameters, instead of focusing on any single parameter, such as cash flow alone, or the 1% ratio.

This chapter covers investing in rental properties. In addition, many people invest in mutual funds. Therefore, the next chapter focuses on how to select mutual funds. The right choice can result in millions of dollars of additional wealth for the ordinary person.

Chapter 15. These Mutual Funds All Look Similar

Myth: **Just pick a few mutual funds and they are all pretty much the same.**

Money Tree: **Simple choice, life-changing difference.**

Arnold Schwarzenegger is a great bodybuilder. He won the Mr. Universe title at age 20. He won the Mr. Olympia contest for a total of seven times. However, wearing a suit and a tie, he looked just like many of the gentlemen next to him. It was when the suit, tie and shirt flew off, when the marvelous muscles of the great bodybuilder were revealed.

Similarly, this chapter and the next chapter will reveal the hidden qualities of mutual funds.

My daughter Sweetie and her husband Moutai asked me how to choose mutual funds to invest in their 401k accounts. Their company gave them a list of choices for their 401k and they were not sure which ones to select.

I told them: "Just keep it simple and put 100% into an S&P 500 index fund. It beats most mutual funds, and has a super low fee of typically around 0.04%."

Besides 401k, many people invest in mutual funds for their regular accounts, as well as IRA and Roth IRA accounts. Some think that mutual funds are similar and they just choose a few to try out. Others chase the "hot" mutual funds to invest in, only to find out that, while these "hot" funds returned a lot last year, their returns deteriorate in subsequent years. How do we choose mutual funds? First, let's look at the S&P 500 index.

1. The S&P 500 Index

There are several main types of equity index funds, including total stock market index funds, S&P 500 index funds, mid cap index funds, small cap index funds, emerging market index funds, growth index funds, value index funds, etc.

While I have been investing in the S&P 500 for two decades, you may choose your favorite index fund or ETF. Just make sure that the funds are as good as, if not better than, the S&P 500. A checklist of criteria is described in Chapter 1.

The S&P 500 stands for Standard & Poor's 500 Index. It is a market-capitalization-weighted index that covers the 500 largest public companies in the United States. S&P 500 index funds are among the most popular index funds.

The S&P 500 goes up and down, with some years increasing by over 30% and other times dropping over 30%.

155

Below is a list of the S&P 500 annual percentage change with dividends included.[1]

S&P 500 Index Annual Return Rate % (Including Dividends)

Year	Rate	Year	Rate	Year	Rate
1965	10.0	1985	31.6	2005	4.9
1966	-11.7	1986	18.6	2006	15.8
1967	30.9	1987	5.1	2007	5.5
1968	11.0	1988	16.6	2008	-37.0
1969	-8.4	1989	31.7	2009	26.5
1970	3.9	1990	-3.1	2010	15.1
1971	14.6	1991	30.5	2011	2.1
1972	18.9	1992	7.6	2012	16.0
1973	-14.8	1993	10.1	2013	32.4
1974	-26.4	1994	1.3	2014	13.7
1975	37.2	1995	37.6	2015	1.4
1976	23.6	1996	23.0	2016	12.0
1977	-7.4	1997	33.4	2017	21.8
1978	6.4	1998	28.6	2018	-4.4
1979	18.2	1999	21.0	2019	31.5
1980	32.3	2000	-9.1	2020	18.4
1981	-5.0	2001	-11.9		
1982	21.4	2002	-22.1		
1983	22.4	2003	28.7		
1984	6.1	2004	10.9		

The Average Compounded Annual Rate of Return of S&P 500 (1965-2020) = 10%.

I include this list here because it is a valuable resource. It provides a vivid impression of how it goes up and down, how some years are much better than others, and nonetheless, in the end, it yields an average of 10% annual return.

This list is important to me as it gives me confidence and strength, and helps me to calmly focus on the math and avoid the emotions, when I pour money into the S&P 500. During market turbulence, or whenever I am in doubt, I take a look at this list, and it calms me down and makes my view clearer.

My wife and I invest in real estate. We also pour some of the cash flow money and cash-out refinance money into the S&P 500. In addition, our 401k is invested in the S&P 500. The S&P 500 returns, listed above, convince me to simply (1) do dollar cost averaging, and (2) hold it for the long-term.

2. Hedge Funds

Most 401k accounts do not provide choices for hedge funds. However, this chapter is applicable not only to 401k investing, but also to regular investing beyond the 401k. Therefore, a discussion on hedge funds is included here.

Mr. Mark Hulbert analyzed the returns for hedge funds from 1994 to 2019.[2] In his analysis, he used the monthly returns of the Credit Suisse Hedge Fund Index. Over the 26 years from 1994-2019, the hedge fund index had an annualized return of 7.8%. The S&P 500 returned 10% annually in average. Therefore, the hedge fund index lagged by 2.2%.

Is a difference of 2.2% a big deal? Let's find out.

Assume that, at age 30, Albert invests $100,000 in an S&P 500 index fund. By age 70, it grows to:

$100,000 x 1.10**40 = $4.5 million.

In comparison, assume that Sam chooses to not use the S&P 500. Assume that, at age 30, Sam invests $100,000 in hedge funds that return 7.8% annually, using the rate of return reported by Mark Hulbert. Then, by age 70, it grows to:

$100,000 x 1.078**40 = $2.0 million.

Ouch, it hurts. By choosing the hedge funds that return 7.8% annually, Sam loses $2.5 million, compared to the simple and passive S&P 500.

The $2.5 million could be a life-changing amount for an ordinary person. Indeed, a simple and easy choice; a life-changing difference.

3. Mutual Funds

Some mutual funds occasionally beat the S&P 500 in a year but then lose in subsequent years. Many mutual fund managers are smart, hard-working and talented experts. However, it is just very difficult to consistently beat the S&P 500 in the long term. When averaged over a time period of 10 years, most of the large cap mutual funds (85% of them) returned less than the S&P 500 index. When the time-frame was increased to 15 years, 92% of the large cap mutual funds returned less than the S&P 500.[3]

According to another report that analyzed the returns for 20 years from 1997 to 2017, investors obtained an average annual return of 4.67% from mutual funds.[4]

In contrast, in the same 20 year period, the S&P 500 returned an average of 8.19% annually.[4]

How much a difference does this make? For illustrative purposes, assume a single investment of $100,000 at the age of 30. Using the aforementioned 4.67% vs. 8.19%, at age 70:

Average mutual funds, $100,000 x 1.0467**40 = $0.62 million.

The S&P 500, $100,000 x 1.0819**40 = $2.33 million.

Instead of obtaining $2.33 million, one gets only $0.62 million investing in average mutual funds. This is a main reason why many ordinary people, including 401k, IRA and Roth IRA investors, stay ordinary financially in their entire life.

If you are a fund manager and you consistently outperform the S&P 500 in the long term, you are a Wall Street star. If you are a small investor picking stocks to invest, and you consistently beat the S&P 500 in the long term, financial firms will be competing to recruit you.

Indeed, the vast majority, 92% to 96%, of all mutual funds failed to outperform their corresponding benchmarks over a time frame of 15 years.[5]

Therefore, for an ordinary person looking for mutual funds to invest in, the S&P 500 is a good and simple choice.

Instead of doing research every year to try to find the mutual funds to beat the S&P 500, you will likely make more money in the long term, and spend less time, sticking with the S&P 500.

4. Is the Conventional Wisdom of "Playing It Safe" Wise?

Let's try to solve a mystery: "Why are most ordinary people with ordinary incomes unable to accumulate millions of dollars in their 401k accounts?"

Employees with 401k accounts typically have a list of funds to choose from. They may allocate their 401k investments in stock funds, bond funds, income-producing funds, and cash-equivalent funds.

Regarding cash-equivalent funds, Mr. Warren Buffett advises: "Today people who hold cash equivalents feel comfortable. They shouldn't. They have opted for a terrible long-term asset, one that pays virtually nothing and is certain to depreciate in value."

Some employees choose to invest in target-date mutual funds for their 401k. The target-date funds use the target date that you plan to retire, and gradually reduce the allocated stock-to-bond ratio. As a result, the rate of return is decreased when you approach your retirement date. For example, in 2020, a 2050-targeted mutual fund may have an annual return of around 8%. In contrast, a 2025-targeted mutual fund may have an annual return of, say, 3%.

"What type of investment do Wall Street traders call a

007? A Bond."

Bonds are useful. Bonds and bond mutual funds have their places. However, their returns are lower than stocks in the long term. Life expectancy is increasing, and there is continued innovation and future developments in medical therapies. People are more likely to live into their 80s, 90s and beyond in the future. Therefore, the intelligent small investor should focus on stocks and emphasize a higher rate of return to build wealth, especially while in their 30s, 40s, 50s and 60s.

According to the analysis of Christine Benz of Morningstar,[6] investors on average get about 5% annual return from their 401K. That is about 5% less than the S&P 500's average annual return of 10%. The reason for the relatively low returns in most 401k accounts is that many people follow the conventional wisdom to "play it safe". They err on the side of caution and are overly conservative.[6]

This can make a huge difference in the end results. Assume a single investment of $100,000 at age 30 (This is a simple estimate to show the important point. Most likely, you will put money into your 401k every two weeks and continue to invest for several decades). Then, at age 70:

Average 401k: $100,000 x 1.05**40 = $0.7 million.
If the 401k investor invested his or her money in the S&P 500:
$100,000 x 1.10**40 = $4.5 million.

Important Point. We have just solved a big mystery.

This is an expensive mystery that has affected millions and millions of ordinary people.

This solves the mystery of why most 401k holders do not accumulate a few million dollars. By "playing it safe", an ordinary investor gets only $0.7 million, instead of $4.5 million that can be harvested passively, by doing nothing.

Conventional wisdom of "playing it safe" can burn millions of dollars into ashes

By "playing it safe", investors actually put their financial situation into an unsafe position. The conventional wisdom of "playing it safe" has robbed them of their financial freedom.

Well-known American psychologist Abraham Maslow said: "In any given moment, we have two options: To step forward into growth or to step back into safety."[7]

By stepping forward into growth, you have the S&P 500 spitting out an extra $3.8 million for you. Imagine how much you and your loved ones can do with the extra $3.8 million.

Therefore, the conventional wisdom of "playing it safe" can burn millions of dollars into ashes.

Indeed, conventional wisdom can kill financial freedom.

Now, let's say that Larry tries to suppress the "playing it safe" mentality. He increases the stock portion in his 401k allocation, thereby increasing his 401k annual return to 6%. Abraham also controls the "playing it safe" emotion and increases his stock exposure, thus raises his annual return to 7%. Meanwhile, Sweetie simply keeps 100% of her 401k in an S&P 500 index fund.

At 6%, Larry will have at age 70: $100,000 x 1.06**40 = $1.0 million.

At 7%, Abraham will have at age 70: $100,000 x 1.07**40 = $1.5 million.

A picture is worth a thousand words. It shows: A simple choice, a big and life-changing financial difference. Indeed, life is the result of our choices.

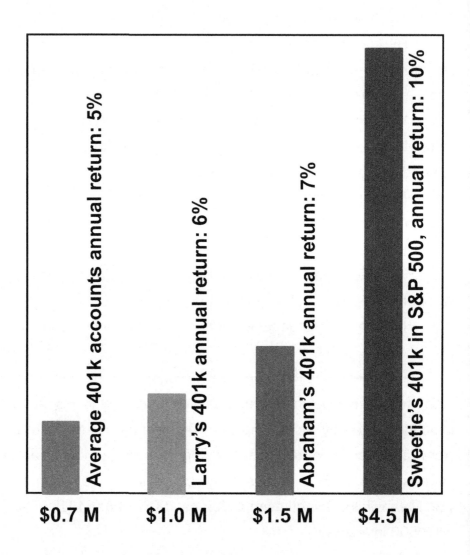

| $0.7 M | $1.0 M | $1.5 M | $4.5 M |

Therefore, this chapter shows that choosing which mutual fund is highly important and can make a life-changing difference. The next chapter will focus another important factor in mutual fund choices: Fees.

Chapter 16. It's Just 1%. What's the Big Deal?

Myth: **A 1% mutual fund fee is no big deal.**

Money Tree: **A 1% mutual fund fee can cost you millions of dollars.**

There is a popular Chinese proverb: "An initial miss of a millimeter eventually leads to a difference of a thousand kilometers." You will agree with this proverb after you read this chapter.

Let me ask: "If you are the owner of a small company, and an employee costs you millions of dollars in lost profits, will you reward him with a $500,000 bonus?"

You would surely answer: "Are you crazy? Of course not!"

Well, wait till you read this chapter.

When choosing mutual funds, the annual fees are an important factor. Mutual fund and hedge fund fees can cost us a significant amount of money. This may catch most people by surprise, because they usually do not think that a seemingly small fund fee, such as 1%, is a big deal.

Is a small 1% fee a big deal?

The fee eats into our money in three ways. (1) It reduces the annual return for the year. (2) Most of these fees are annual, so the fund managers charge us, say, 1% every year. After a decade or two, with the growth of our money, that 1% fee is also taking away a larger and larger sum of our money. (3) It reduces our compounding power. Remember, compounding is the eighth wonder of the world.

1. Good Mutual Funds

To illustrate the point, simply assume that you invest a one-time $100,000 at the age of 30 into a mutual fund. It charges a 1% fee. By the time you retire at the age of 70, it's been 40 years.

Assume that you choose a good mutual fund that returns a decent 9% annually on average in those 40 years (there are plenty of mutual funds that do worse). After the 1% fee, you get a net 8% return (again, 8% annually compounding for 40 years is quite decent among the mutual funds. Many mutual funds do worse than this.) After 40 years, your initial investment of $100,000 becomes:

$100,000 x 1.08**40 = $2.17 million.

Do not be surprised by this large number. It will be worth much less in purchasing power after 40 years, due to inflation.

However, what happens if you use the S&P 500 instead?

Assume that you put the $100,000 into a S&P 500 index fund that charges a relatively negligible fee of 0.04% (I have all my mutual fund money in such a fund). The average annual return was 10% for S&P 500 (1965-2019). After 40 years, your initial investment of $100,000 becomes:

$100,000 x 1.10**40 = $4.53 million.

This is $2.36 million more than what the good mutual fund produces.

By choosing a good mutual fund instead of the simple and low-fee S&P 500, the investor loses $2.36 million.

Please note the following. (1) This estimate assumes a single investment at age 30. You likely will be putting more money into it each year throughout your working life. This means that the loss from using the good mutual fund will be even bigger than the $2.36 million. (2) If you are among a higher income group such as doctors and dentists, or have more money such as from a family inheritance, you will likely invest much more than $100,000. This means that you would lose much more than $2.36 million, by using a good mutual fund over the S&P 500. (3) This example uses a good mutual fund that returns 9% before fees for over 40 years. Most mutual funds cannot match this, which means that you would lose even more money. Point # 3 is further discussed below.

2. Average Mutual Funds

Instead of a good mutual fund, now let's look at the average mutual fund.

Although many mutual fund managers are highly educated and work diligently, history and statistics have proven that beating the unmanaged S&P 500 index is a daunting task. In addition, the mutual fund expenses eat into the returns.

Many people spread their investments over several mutual funds, such as 5 or 6 funds, or a dozen funds. The net result is that they usually obtain an overall rate of return that represents the mutual fund average.

Mutual funds charge fees to pay for the salaries and bonuses of fund managers and investment advisors, as well as the expenses of marketing, shareholder services, accounting, legal, and other administrative activities.

I am not against mutual fund fees. I don't mind paying a 1% fee or a 0.75% fee to a mutual fund or a hedge fund, if it can outperform the S&P 500 after the fees. If the fund managers increase my rate of return, then they deserve my fees. However, if they underperform the index fund, then I would rather invest in the index fund to protect my hard-earned money.

First, what are average mutual fund fees? Deborah Fowles has written a helpful article about mutual funds fees.[1] The article was updated in May 2020, hence this was recent information. It states that "The average mutual fund expense ratio is between 1.3-1.5%."

Second, what is the average annual return for mutual funds? A report showed that in 15 years from 2004-2019, the mean rate of return per year for mutual funds was 6.02%.[2]

The average mutual funds underperform the S&P 500 before fees. And then they charge hefty fees. This double whammy leads to a mean rate of return of 6.02% for the mutual funds.

A single investment of $100,000 at age 30 will become how much at age 70?

Average mutual funds with 6.02% return: $100,000 x 1.0602**40 = $1.04 million.

S&P 500 index fund with 10% return: $100,000 x 1.10**40 = $4.53 million.

The average mutual funds lose $3.49 million in profits, compared to the passive S&P 500.

Let's go back to the illustration in which you are the owner of a small company. In this example, your employee loses $3.49 million in profits for you.

Do you then reward this employee by giving him or her a big bonus? Let's see below.

3. Mutual Fund Fees

Over an investment lifetime, how much money does an average investor give to the fund manager in the form of mutual fund fees? Dayana Yochim and Jonathan Todd analyzed how much mutual fund fees can cost the investors.[3] In one of the scenarios, they made a calculation based on paying mutual fund fees of just 1% (which most people may be tricked into thinking that it's not a big deal). Over 40 years, this fee would cost a typical millennial investor greater than $590,000.

Over 40 years, a typical millennial pays fees to the fund managers that cost the millennial $590,000.

Using this example, if a mutual fund fee of 1% costs $590,000 over 40 years to a typical investor, then let's simply estimate that an S&P 500 index fund, with a fee of 0.04%, would cost $590,000 x 0.04 = $23,600.

The difference is $590,000 - $23,600 = $566,400. The typical millennial would have saved $566,400 if s/he has invested in the S&P 500 due to savings from the fees alone.

Therefore, most people invest in typical and average mutual funds, and lose $3.49 million in sacrificed returns (using the example above, over 40 years, compared to the S&P 500). In addition, they generously hand over hefty fees to the fund managers and brokers that cost the investor $590,000, to reward the fund managers and brokers for losing millions of the investor's money.

The following saying applies to fees charged by brokers

in trading options.[4] It similarly applies to fees charged by hedge funds and mutual funds:

"I put two children through Harvard by trading options. Unfortunately, they were my broker's children."

Indeed, mutual funds are not mutual. For example, if the mutual fund drops by 20%, the investor eats the 20% loss. On the other hand, the fund managers continue to receive profits in the form of fees.

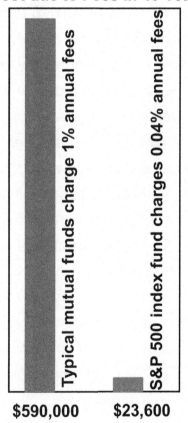

Your Wealth in 40 Years		Cost due to Fees in 40 Years	
Average mutual fund with 6.02% annual return	S&P 500 index fund with 10% annual return	Typical mutual funds charge 1% annual fees	S&P 500 index fund charges 0.04% annual fees
$1.04 M	$4.53 M	$590,000	$23,600

To drive home the point, imagine that you are the boss and you need to hire an employee. You face two candidates.

Applicant A is excellent. Applicant F would lose you millions of dollars in the years to come, and yet F wants a higher salary, which over the years would cost you an extra of $566,400, than A.

Would you hire A or F?

Of course, you would hire A.

Unfortunately, when it comes to investing in mutual funds as well as 401k and IRA accounts, most people hire F. This is because they do not look at the math. They are tricked by the fancy brochures and attractive advertisements of mutual funds. In addition, people are tricked into believing that this active strategy of mutual fund X, or that complicated approach of mutual fund Y, are better than the passive "do-nothing" S&P 500 which may seem too simple and unexciting.

I hope this book will serve as a wake-up call to people.

I hope this chapter will benefit many families. Reading this chapter takes only half an hour. Yet it can make an ordinary family several million dollars in additional wealth.

I do not run funds to invest other people's money. I do not want to invest your money and charge you fees. Your choices of mutual funds do not benefit me. I have no conflict of interest. This information is to the benefit of you, the reader, and your loved ones.

The Money Tree Way. If you want to invest in mutual funds, whether for your 401k, IRA and Roth IRA or regular accounts, simply put your money into an S&P 500 index fund. You may also choose another similarly good index fund of your choice. This will grow millions of dollars more than the average mutual funds over your working life, plus saving you half a million dollars due to fund fees.

You may say: "Wow, I did not know that mutual fund fees can cost me so much! I will not use these mutual funds. I will pick individual stocks and invest by myself." That is the topic of the next chapter.

Chapter 17. Work Harder and Lose Money?

Myth: **I can pick stocks to invest and beat the market.**

Money Tree: **Spend less time and make millions more.**

There is a joke about a day-trader whose mind was absorbed into the stock market with the news and ups and downs. He was standing in the hallway outside of his office and forgot where he was going. He scratched his head and asked himself:

"Was I walking toward the man's room? Or did I already finish the man's room and was walking back to my office?"

That seems to be quite a stressful lifestyle. Some people like it. A small number of day-traders do well.

However, for the majority of people, the question is: "Is there an easier way to invest?"

The answer is yes. There is an easy way. It is so easy that you may call it "do-nothing", or inaction. And it makes your more money. A lot more.

This is the focus of this chapter.

1. Individual Stories

A few years ago, I was in China visiting my parents and other relatives. One relative gave birth to a baby, so I went over to give the young couple a red envelope to congratulate them. In China, when people get married, have babies, or celebrate birthdays, a common way to congratulate them is to give them a red envelope that contains a cash gift.

While there, we chatted, and the conversation moved to investing. The husband said: "This year, two of my businesses are doing well. However, my stock market investments have lost 400,000 yuan." For reference, in the fall of 2020, $1 was equal to 6.6 yuan.

Before I could find words to comfort him over his loss, my other relative, who drove me to see this young couple, quickly said: "That's OK. I have lost more. I have lost over 700,000 yuan trading stocks."

According to them, it is popular for people there to pick individual stocks to invest in, and they usually buy and sell quite frequently. A few of them make a lot of money. Most of them make little money or lose some money. A few of them lose big and are wiped out.

Back in America, my wife and I know a friendly lady, Melinda. For years, she was picking individual stocks to invest in. She spent a lot of time siting with a computer, for such a long time that it hurt her eyes. According to herself, some time she won big, other times she lost big. Overall, she made little money, similar to what CDs returned, a few percentages per year. She said: "It's not worth it." Eventually, she quit trading stocks and found something else to do.

We have another friend, Ron, who is highly intelligent and has a PhD degree. During a conversation, he said that years ago when he was trading stocks, he lost about $100,000. "It was brutal and stressful," he sighed.

I had a colleague, Caleb, years ago. He bought and sold stocks and used puts and calls. One day, during a Powerpoint presentation in the conference room with coworkers, he accidentally showed the screen of his stock symbols and everyone laughed. A couple years later, I caught up with him and the topic went to investing. I asked: "How is your stock investing going?" He did not seem excited: "Oh, I am pretty much at breakeven."

As people say: "The stock market is weird. Every time one guy sells, another one buys, and they both think they're smart."

At least Caleb did not lose money. But he spent a lot of time with little to show.

I had another colleague, Galvan, who was relatively wealthy among the colleagues. He had quite some money to invest and used a financial firm. One day at work, a well-dressed gentleman came to his office while I was also there.

Galvan introduced to me that this gentleman was his financial advisor from the investment firm. Since Galvan had a significant amount of money with this firm, they sent a financial advisor to meet with him from time to time to go over his investments. In addition, the firm made recommendations such as to buy this stock or to sell that stock via emails and phone calls to him.

Later, I asked Galvan: "What kind of annual returns have you been getting from using your financial advisor?" Galvin replied: "Well, it's usually about 7-8% per year."

That beats many stock traders. But that is 2-3% below the passive S&P 500.

2. Statistical Observations from Published Articles

The main challenges facing individual stock investors and traders include: Chasing hot stocks and buying high, selling low during a panic, managing emotions, overreacting to short-term news, frequent trading, or "inside" tips from Uncle Doug or from colleague Carol, etc.

According to Mr. Charlie Cameron: "The average person does far worse than the market overall average returns."[1] Therefore, the suggestion is that the best way for any average person to make money in the stock market is to invest in simple stock index funds, such as an S&P 500 index fund.

Indeed, most individual stock traders do not succeed. According to the article "Scientist Discovered Why Most

177

Traders Lose Money - 24 Surprising Statistics", the most commonly-used trading-related statistic around the internet shows that 95% of all traders fail. It shows that while all traders start with a dream of getting rich, 80% of them quit in the first two years. Only 1% of all traders make a significant profit.[2]

In a Forbes article, Neale Godfrey shows: "The success rate for day traders is estimated to be around only 10%, so ... 90% of them are losing money." "Only 1% of day traders really make (significant amounts of) money."[3]

Indeed, as Mr. Warren Buffett said: "The stock market is designed to transfer money from the active to the patient."

3. The Chance of Consistently Beating the Market Is Tiny

A few gifted and lucky individuals do well in stock investing; congratulations to them. I respect them. However, they are among a very small percentage.

Some people trade stocks as a hobby. That is fine, if you treat it as a hobby and not as a way to grow your wealth. Just bear in mind that most people will underperform equity index funds. Only a very small percentage of investors can consistently outperform the S&P 500 in the long term.

Some folks like to gamble and they trade stocks to satisfy their gambling interest. A certain percentage of people like to gamble. Some gamble in Las Vegas. Others do sports gambling. That is fine. Just play with the money that you can afford to lose. Keep the following joke in mind:[4]

178

"I tell my father's story of the gambler who lost regularly. One day he heard about a race with only one horse in it. He thought: 'That horse will surely be the winner.' So he bet the family ranch on it. Halfway around the track, the horse jumped over the fence and ran away."

Another important factor to consider is whether an investment could move the needle to increase my wealth or not. For example, if I were to invest in an individual stock, I may dare to invest, say, only $20,000 in one company's stock. Then even if it doubles, I make only $20,000 profit. I would not dare to put a lot of money into a single company's stock. Therefore, the profit would not significantly move the needle to increase my wealth. However, it would take a lot of my time and effort to do research and to select a company.

It gives me stress to select companies to invest significant amounts of my money. Companies can go bankrupt, and their stock prices can go to 0 and never recover. In contrast, the S&P 500 will not go to 0, and it have always recovered from any dips. If a company inside the S&P 500 index performs sufficiently poorly, that company will be dropped out of the S&P 500 index. And a new and better company will enter into the S&P 500 index.

With the S&P 500, I dare to pour $1 million or more into it, and hold it for the long term. With real estate, I am willing to put in all the money that I have, plus all the money that I can borrow, as long as the deals satisfy my safeguards. These are the advantages of the S&P 500 and real estate investing. I can use large amounts of money and go all in. I can grow our money trees at a relatively large scale. This yields significant profits in the long term.

These actions can move the needle to significantly increase our family wealth.

In addition, in stock investing, the most important organ is the stomach, not the brain. For example, even if someone bought Amazon stocks in 1997, they face three challenges. (1) Most small investors do not have the stomach to hold it for over twenty years. Most will sell when their money doubles or triples. (2) Many people will sell when it drops 30% or 50%. Amazon has dropped over 30% and 50% multiple times. In its worst crash, it lost 94% of its value. With forecasters and commentators using the word "bankruptcy", how many people can hold on to this stock? (3) Back then, such as in 1997 or 2001, most small investors did not have the stomach to put a lot of money into Amazon. A small amount of money, even if it is doubles or triples, will not move the needle of his or her total wealth. It will not result in financial freedom for the majority of ordinary people.

The percentage of people who put in a large chunk of his or her wealth into Amazon in 2001 and then hold it without selling for two decades, is very small. It probably approaches the small percentage of people winning the lottery.

Therefore, being able to go all in, and being able to significantly move the needle to grow our family wealth, are two important aspects of my considerations.

4. Your Money Is Like a Soap Bar

Some people spend a lot of time in stock trading and still cannot consistently beat the S&P 500 in the long term. Some may gamble and win big in one year, but then lose it in the next year or two.

Frequent trading is stressful, and it does not help in achieving financial freedom. It actually reduces the rate of return. Too many actions, the pursuit of excitement, and the chase of hot stocks can seriously hurt the performance.

Indeed, as Benjamin Graham said:

"The investor's chief problem - and even his worst enemy - is likely to be himself."[5]

By investing in the S&P 500 and then forgetting about it, I remove "myself" from interfering with the investment.

In addition, it is important to have a good quality of life and to have plenty of time with my family.

There is really no need to make life so stressful. As Warren Buffett said:

"You only have to do a very few things right in your life so long as you don't do too many things wrong."[6]

Doing too many things and being stressful can be counterproductive.

I ask myself: "Am I among the top 1% in selecting individual stocks?" The answer is no.

"Do I want to compete with Wall Street experts who play

golf with the CEOs and have dinners with the CFOs?" No.

"Do I have the time and expertise to research the companies?" No.

"Do I want to endure the ups and downs and the associated mood swings?" No.

Personally, for me, with real estate, I delegate as much of the duties as possible to my team. With stock market, I put money into an S&P 500 index fund and then forget about it. I do dollar cost averaging, and hold it for the long term. I look at it only once a year when I record the year-end annual report.

The reason for using a good index fund is that it is simple and trouble-free. You dump the money into it and then forget about it. It is not like trading stocks which may keep you busy and stressful all day, and keep you awake at night.

The economist Gene Fama Jr. said:

"Your money is like a bar of soap. The more you handle it, the less you'll have."[7]

Trading stocks takes a lot of actions, especially if you are a short-term trader. It increases the stress level, which is known to be a carcinogen. It compromises the quality of life.

In comparison, investing in a good index fund via dollar cost averaging and then holding it for the long term would be like "doing nothing". It is basically inaction. However, in this case, inaction is the best action.

The "do-nothing" method can serve the ordinary people well. Even for investing geniuses like Warren Buffett, he quipped that some of his best investment actions were sitting on his ass and doing nothing.

5. Summary: Less Work, More Wealth

As described in this chapter, Galvan used a financial advisor and his annual return was 7-8% (Let's use the middle point of 7.5% in the following calculation). Assume that a single $100,000 is invested at age 30. Assume that he sells it at age 70. From age 30 to 70 is 40 years. It yields:

Galvan uses a financial advisor: $100,000 x 1.075**40 = $1.80 million.

The intelligent small investor uses S&P 500 passively "doing-nothing": $100,000 x 1.10**40 = $4.53 million.

This Table summarizes the examples and illustrations of this chapter.

Investor	Results	Time Spent
Melinda	2-3% return	Frequent trading
Ron	Lost $100,000	Frequent trading
Caleb	Breakeven	Frequent trading
Galvan	$1.80 million	Use financial advisor
The Intelligent Small Investor	*$4.53 million*	*Do nothing*

This chapter compares the money tree methods with various traditional approaches that individual small investors have employed. It can be summarized with this money tree motto:

"Less Work, More Wealth (LWMW)."

The next chapter further compares the money tree methods with starting a business and running a company.

Chapter 18. This Sounds Too Easy to Be True

Myth: Start a business and work really hard to get rich.

Money Tree: Intelligent small investors spend less time and outperform most startups and big companies.

We often say: "If something sounds too good to be true, it probably isn't true." This chapter will show you something that sounds too easy to be true, but is actually true.

1. Only a Small Percentage of People Do Very Well by Starting Businesses

My friend Jill started a biotech company a decade ago. She not only is excellent at biomedical sciences, but also is highly talented at networking, marketing and raising capital. She worked very hard for nearly 10 years, and her product finally won the FDA approval. In 2019, Jill sold her company and retired. She donated $5 million to her former university, and had a research center there named after her. She says that she now focuses on charity, dance and travel. Jill has done very well. Congratulations to her.

Jill is exceptional. New entrepreneurs who start businesses face many challenges. I have another friend, a capable gentleman, who started his own company. He poured his money and time into the company, and for a while the company did quite well. Then after several years, the business declined and he had to close shop. He found a job and went back to work to support his family with three kids.

Indeed, only a small percentage of people succeed in starting businesses and companies. I talked with several local friends who knew businesses well. They said that roughly, only 1 in 10 who started businesses would succeed.

Their number is consistent with reports that show that an estimated 90% of new startups fail.[1] Therefore, only 10% of them will avoid the fate of failure. However, even if they avoid the fate of failure, but return, say, only 5% or 7% of the invested capital, then they are still underperforming the passive, do-nothing S&P 500. The percentage of these companies that outperform the S&P 500 is even less than 10%.

Therefore, in most cases, people who start companies and businesses either fail, or return less than simply dumping the money into a good, passive index fund.

I have a lot of respect for entrepreneurs who start companies. They hire people and provide services that benefit the society. A few of them eventually succeed and do very well. However, in terms of the rate of return on the invested capital, by simply investing in the S&P 500, I have a greater than 90% chance of growing wealth faster than I would by working days, nights, and weekends starting my own business.

If you have the ambition to start your own business, please go head. You have my admiration and respect. I don't want this chapter to discourage you. This country needs entrepreneurs, and some of them succeed and do very well.

For most ordinary people, we may not have the time, will and expertise to start our own businesses. Still, we can rest assured that our simple investments in an equity index fund or in rental houses in our own neighborhoods would do well in the long term. The simple money tree methods of this book can actually far exceed the returns of most startups.

2. Even for the Big Guys, the Return Is Often Greater by Dumping the Money into an Equity Index Fund

It is said that "It takes brains to make millions. It takes Trump to make billions." Indeed, Mr. Donald J. Trump has done well in real estate, and *Forbes* estimated his wealth at $3.5 billion in 2017. It was reported in *MarketWatch* in 2017 that Trump had $200 million in 1974, and his wealth grew to $3.5 billion in 2017. That corresponded to a rate of return of 6.9% annually. It underperformed the S&P 500 index.

Indeed, if he had simply dumped that $200 million in an

equity index fund in 1974, he would have had more than $15 billion by 2017, instead of $3.5 billion.[2]

Therefore, based on these reports, Mr. Trump would have been at least $10 billion richer if he had simply kept his money in a passive, "do-nothing", S&P 500 index fund.

Mr. Trump worked hard and slept only 4 hours per day, according to himself. He said: "If I sleep only 4 hours a day, and you sleep 10 hours, how can you compete with me?"

Yes, Mr. Trump creates jobs and employs a lot of people. There are benefits to the country and to the society.

However, when it comes to the rate of return and the specific goal of achieving financial freedom for the ordinary family, it is more rewarding to stick with an equity index fund for the majority of the small investors. This is especially so, when you consider the high failure rate and the busy working schedule in running a company.

The Oracle of Omaha Warren Buffett wisely said: "I don't look to jump over seven-foot bars; I look around for one-foot bars that I can step over."

For a small potato like me, personally, to undertake a start-up company would be like to jump over a seven-foot bar. In contrast, the one-foot bars are the rental houses in my own backyard and the S&P 500 index.

3. Even Business Gurus Can't Guarantee that Running a Company Returns More Than Investing in an Index Fund

Mr. Warren Buffett is one of the most famous investors of all time. He and Charlie Munger lead Berkshire Hathaway, one of the top companies in the world. They work very hard. I read in books that say that Buffett and Munger read many quarterly statements of companies regularly, as well as dozens of trading and business journals, magazines and newspapers on a daily basis. These are in addition to spending time and efforts to direct a large company that includes dozens of sub-companies. They are highly intelligent, extremely capable, hard-working and efficient business leaders.

According to the Berkshire Hathaway's annual reports, Buffett's rate of return from 1965-1999 exceeded the S&P 500 mainly due to his extraordinary returns in the early years of his career. Lately, his rate of return either matched or trailed that of the S&P 500. For example, in the last decade, from 2011-2019, Berkshire Hathaway's average annual return was 13.2%. In comparison, in the same time period, the S&P 500 returned 14.1%. The 13.2% return beats most mutual funds and hedge funds, and is nothing to sneeze at.

However, this does indicate the benefit of using a simple equity index fund for ordinary investors. For a small investor like me, investing in the S&P 500 does not require much time, effort, or business expertise. And yet the rate of return beats even the famous Buffett over the past decade.

The business geniuses work hard and deal with numerous challenges in running a company. In the end, regarding the rate of return in growing the wealth for a small investor and the ordinary person, it is not necessarily better than simply putting the money into the "do-nothing" S&P 500.

4. The Intelligent Small Investor

The figure shows annual returns for investments. The last three bars are for the same time period of 2011-2019, for a fair comparison. The last bar for the small investor represents the average annual rate in wealth growth for my wife and I.

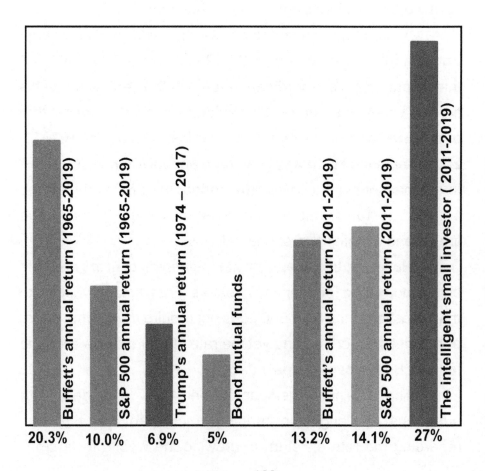

Buffett's annual return (1965-2019)	S&P 500 annual return (1965-2019)	Trump's annual return (1974 – 2017)	Bond mutual funds	Buffett's annual return (2011-2019)	S&P 500 annual return (2011-2019)	The intelligent small investor (2011-2019)
20.3%	10.0%	6.9%	5%	13.2%	14.1%	27%

The returns for Mr. Buffett and the S&P 500 are obtained from.[3] The return for Mr. Trump is adopted from.[2] The return for small investor (my wife and I) is obtained from.[4]

Therefore, (1) simply putting money into an equity index fund beats many big gurus. Ordinary people can accumulate wealth faster by dumping money into an equity index fund. (2) Real estate can further increase the return. Some of our real estate deals yield greater than 25% annual return.

By using a team, I spend only 2-3 hours on real estate per week. In addition, my S&P 500 investing takes little time per year. The money tree methods saves me a lot of valuable time.

As Margaret Bonnano said: "Being rich is having money; being wealthy is having time."[5]

Time is one of the most precious things in life. The money tree methods of this book produce greater returns and require less time. This sounds too good to be true, but it is true. It seems too easy to grow wealth this way, but it is true. For most ordinary people and small investors, the easiest and simplest way is also the best and most lucrative way.

The preceding chapters present money tree methods for high school and college students, young professionals, homeowners, mutual fund investors, 401k and IRA investors, and middle-aged employees. The next chapter presents methods to further grow wealth by 10x after the age of 50.

Chapter 19. Another 10X to Your Wealth

Myth: **By age 50, you should have already made the bulk of your money.**

Money Tree: **Grow your wealth by another 10x after age 50.**

You have read the preceding chapters and are excited. However, you may say: "These all sound great! But I am 50 years old. It is too late for me, right?"

"I am 50 so I should rely on what I already have, and wind down my investments in the near future, right?"

If your net worth is $500,000 at age 50, do you believe that this book can help you grow it to $5 million after age 50?

If you net worth is $3 million at age 50, do you believe that this book can help you grow it to $30 million after age 50?

If you have doubts, this chapter is for you. Of course, the profitable principles and the highly rewarding methods of this chapter also apply if you are 55 years old, or 45, or 35.

1. The Humble Story of My Wife And I

I came to the Unites States in 1988 to attend graduate school. My wife joined me a year later and began her graduate degree. We both started working in 1993. Our first child was born in 1995, the second in 1998, and the third in 2000. We worked hard and saved money diligently. By 2011, we had a net worth of about $800,000, including the equity in our only house, 401k accounts, some mutual funds, and bank accounts. We were busy working and raising our three kids, and paid little attention to investing.

Then my oldest daughter Sweetie got seriously sick following a misdiagnosis. After being hospitalized for 21 days, she thankfully finally recovered. This incident served as a wake-up call, and I started to buy rental houses for the family's financial security.

This experience was detailed in my first book *$5 Million in 8 Years: Real Estate Investing on the Side*. By relying on a team, I spent only a few hours per week on real estate. Our net worth increased from $0.8 million in 2011 to $5.5 million in 2019. This represented an annual rate of 27% in our net worth accumulation. In addition, the net positive cash flow from our rental properties reached $150,000 per year in 2019.

In the coming years, I expect our annual rate of wealth accumulation to be lower than 27%. This is because while our base amount has increased, our leverage has decreased, and it is not easy to obtain further loans from the banks.

Assume that we increase our wealth by 15% annually from now on till the age of 70, which is currently 15 years away. Then, at age 70, our net worth would become:

$5.5 million x 1.15**15 = $44.75 million.

When we were 50 years old, our record showed that we had a net worth of $2.3 million.

Therefore, based on the numbers above, from age 50 to 70, we would grow our wealth by 44.75/2.3 = 19x.

Therefore, from age 50 to 70, we would grow our wealth by 19-fold.

Now let's assume an even lower rate of 12% annually for my wife and I in the next 15 years. The S&P 500 has returns 10% annually in the long-term. Our real estate portfolio with leverage is expected to return significantly more than the S&P 500. We returned 27% from 2011-2019. Hence, 12% per year is expected to be conservative. Then

$5.5 million x 1.12**15 = $30.10 million.

Important Point. This more conservative case assumes a 12% annual return in the future years. From age 50 to 70, my wife and I would grow our wealth by 30.10/2.3 = 13x. We would grow our wealth by 13-fold.

2. You Can Do It Too

For illustrative purposes, assume that you have an investable fund of $1 million at the age of 50. Do not put it in CDs. Do not put it in bonds. Let's look at the following three scenarios.

First Scenario. At age 50, with an investable fund of $1 million, Matt starts to buy rental houses. His annual rate of return is 20%, a little lower than the 27% in my first book, to be on the conservative side in our estimate here. Matt continues for 20 years till age 70, then he sells the rental properties. How much would Matt's $1 million investment have grown?

$1 million x 1.20**20 = $38.34 million.

From age 50 to 70, Matt grows his wealth by 38x.

How much percentage of wealth does Matt make after the age of 50?
(38.34 - 1)/38.34 = 97.4%.

When Matt is 70 years old and retired, and is sipping wine on a cruise ship with his wife and some friends, he looks back and says:
"Wow, I made 97.4% of my wealth after age 50. From when I started to work at age 22 till age 50, I made only 2.6%

of my wealth. Back then when I was 50, I thought that I had already made the bulk of my wealth in my life, and I was ready to put my cool million into CDs and bonds. That little book by David Meng really changed my life!"

Second Scenario. At age 50, Cathy divides her $1 million investment to be partly in rental houses and partly in the S&P 500. Her real estate returns around 20% and her S&P 500 returns around 10%, in average, in the long term. Her overall annual rate of return is an intermediate 15%. How much would her $1 million investment grow when she reaches 70 years of age?

$1 million x 1.15**20 = $16.37 million.

From age 50 to 70, Cathy grows her wealth by 16x.

(16.37 - 1)/16.37 = 93.9%
Hence, Cathy makes 93.9% of her wealth after age 50.

Third Scenario. At age 50, Jack puts his $1 million into the S&P 500, because he does not want to deal with rental houses. His annual rate of return is 10%. How much would his $1 million investment grow when he reaches age 70?

$1 million x 1.10**20 = $6.73 million.

From age 50 to 70, Jack grows his wealth by 6.73x.

(6.73 - 1)/6.73 = 85.1%

Therefore, Jack makes 85.1% of his wealth after age 50.

If you read the previous chapters in this book about avoiding CDs, bonds, income types of mutual funds, as well as other high-fees mutual funds, and simply put your money into the S&P 500 or similarly good index equity funds, and then do nothing, you would still be able to make 85% of your wealth after the age of 50.

You do not have to take the trouble to analyze and select stocks, you do not have to endure the stress of day-trading, you do not have to touch rental properties, and you can still grow your wealth by 6.73x after age 50.

Furthermore, this calculation ends at age 70. With the increase in life expectancy and people living well into their 80s and 90s in the future, Jack can continue with the S&P 500 for another 5 or 10 years, and not sell it all at age 70.

For example, assume that Jack has social security and other reserves to live on, so that he does not sell his S&P 500 at age 70. Instead, he sells his S&P 500 at age 75. From age 50 to 75 is 25 years. How much does his S&P 500 grow to when Jack is 75 years old?

$1 million x 1.10**25 = $10.83 million.

From age 50 to 75, Jack grows his wealth by 10.83x.

(10.83 - 1)/10.83 = 90.8%

Therefore, Jack makes 90.8% of his wealth after age 50.

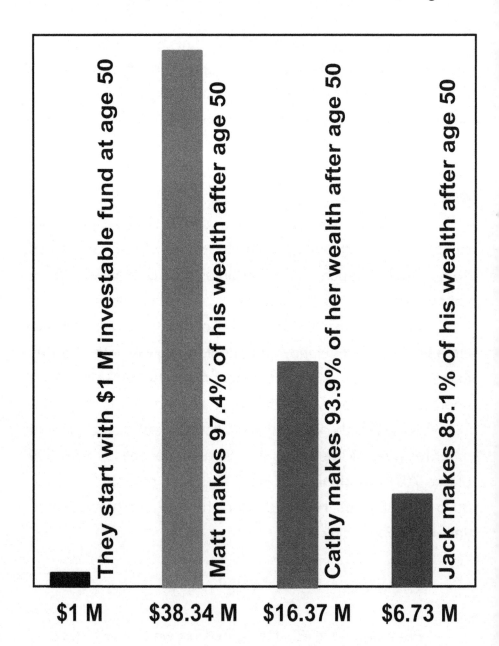

They start with $1 M investable fund at age 50

Matt makes 97.4% of his wealth after age 50

Cathy makes 93.9% of her wealth after age 50

Jack makes 85.1% of his wealth after age 50

$1 M $38.34 M $16.37 M $6.73 M

In the plot, M = million. Each person starts with $1 million at age 50. After 20 years, they sell their investments at age 70.

3. Don't Let Anyone Tell You that You Are Too Old to Do This

Therefore, you can earn the majority of your wealth by investing, even if you start late. Don't let "I am old", "It's too late", or other excuses stop you. Of course, the younger you are when you start investing, the better. Remember that compounding over time is the eighth wonder of the world. Therefore, pull the trigger and do not wait. The best time to start investing was a decade ago. The second best time to start investing is now.

Do not let anyone tell you that you are too old to do this. The age of 50 is not the end. It is not even the beginning of the end. It is only the end of the beginning.

The money tree methods will enable you to achieve financial freedom. You can retire comfortably knowing that you have financial security for yourself and your loved ones.

Once you do retire, and you live a long retired life, will you consume and burn out all your wealth during retirement? Can the money tree methods further grow your wealth in retirement? The next chapter addresses this important topic.

Chapter 20. Make More Money Passively in Your Retirement than Working Hard at a Job

Myth: **After you retire, move money to CDs, bonds and mutual funds, and rebalance annually.**

Money Tree: **Two years of living expenses in cash, all other investments in S&P 500.**

1. I Have a Lucrative and Unorthodox Money Tree Method

"No hurries. No worries. I am retired!"

We all want to enjoy life and avoid the "hurry and worry". How do we grow our money trees in a stress-free and effortless way during retirement?

I have studied more than a hundred books on investing and personal finance, and I have experimented with several investing methods suitable for a stress-free retirement. I have come up with the following money tree method that I believe is highly lucrative, while requiring the least time and effort.

Retired! No bosses, no stress, no hurries, no worries!

When my wife and I retire, we plan to sell our rental properties and invest in S&P 500, leaving two years of living expenses in cash in the bank. Instead of the S&P 500, you may choose your own favorite funds by following a checklist of selection criteria (Chapter 1). If you find a fund with long-term performance better than the S&P 500, feel free to use that fund.

Money Tree Allocation in Retirement: Two years of living expenses in cash + all other investments in the S&P 500.

This chapter explains why this money tree allocation is

highly lucrative, while requiring the least time and effort.

Differences. I understand that people are different and we have different retirement plans and investment choices. We can look at a million snowflakes and they are all unique. This chapter illustrates what I plan to do when the time comes for my wife and I to retire. You may adopt this money tree method, or you may make modifications to it. For example, instead of two years of living expenses in cash, you may prefer to have six months of living expenses in cash, plus eighteen months of living expenses in bonds. Or, perhaps you prefer to be more conservative and want to have three or more years of living expenses in cash or in bonds. Even with these modifications, the outcome is still the same: The money tree method produces much more than conventional methods during your retirement.

Regarding when to retire, different families have different situations. For those who invest in real estate or use the "do-nothing" method as described in this book (Chapters 12 and 13), they have the option to choose to retire in their 40s.

Some other people may choose to retire in the 50s. Still others may choose to retire in their 60s.

For illustrative purposes, the following examples assume that they retire at the age of 50, with an investable asset of $3 million. This is the money that can be invested; this does not include their primary residence or vacation homes or cars. In addition, it is assumed that their houses and cars are paid for without loans, to make the following calculation simpler to illustrate. However, if you prefer to include loans for the calculation, that is also fine; just allocate more than the $80,000 for their annual living expense to account for the mortgage payments. Then use the same living expense number for a fair comparison between the myths and the money tree method.

In addition, the following examples are somewhere in the middle of the potential range. Some families may retire with more than $3 million, and some may have less. You may have $1 million, or you may have $10 million. You can still make the comparison between the myths and the money tree method using the same procedures as described below, while substituting with your own investable amount and age.

2. Money Tree Method - Two Years' Living Expense in Cash, All Else in S&P 500

Amy and Adam retire at the age of 50. They have an investable wealth amount of $3 million. They live in an ordinary American town with average living expenses, which indicate that they need $80,000 per year to pay for their living expenses.

Using the method of putting two years of living expenses as cash in the bank, Amy and Adam put $160,000 in their bank account. The rest, $2,840,000, they put into the S&P 500.

Long-term historical data from 1965-2019 show that, in average, the S&P 500 has returned 10% annually.

Every year in January, Amy and Adam sell $80,000 of their S&P 500 and deposit it into their bank account to replenish and maintain their $160,000 cash reserve.

How much money will they have after 20 years when they reach age 70? Will this money tree method grow more money for them while they enjoy their retirement?

Year 0, they have $160,000 cash in the bank, and $2,840,000 in the S&P 500.

Year 1, they spend $80,000, and sell $80,000 of the S&P 500 to add to their bank account to maintain two years of living expenses in cash.

Year 1, their S&P 500 amount = $2,840,000 x 1.10 (it grows by 10% annually) - $80,000 (the selling) = $3,044,000.

Year 2, they do the same thing as year 1. They spend $80,000, and sell $80,000 of the S&P 500 to add to their bank account. Their S&P 500 amount = $3,044,000 x 1.10 - $80,000 = $3,268,400.

Year 3, their S&P 500 = $3,268,400 x 1.10 - $80,000 = $3,515,240.

Year 4, their S&P 500 = $3,515,240 x 1.10 - $80,000 = $3,786,764.

Year 5, their S&P 500 = $3,786,764 x 1.10 - $80,000 = $4,085,440.

Year 6, their S&P 500 = $4,085,440 x 1.10 - $80,000 = $4,413,984.

Year 7, their S&P 500 = $4,413,984 x 1.10 - $80,000 = $4,775,383.

Year 8, their S&P 500 = $4,775,383 x 1.10 - $80,000 = $5,192,921.

Year 9, their S&P 500 = $5,192,921 x 1.10 - $80,000 = $5,610,213.

Year 10, their S&P 500 = $5,610,213 x 1.10 - $80,000 = $6,091,235.

Year 11, their S&P 500 = $6,091,235 x 1.10 - $80,000 = $6,620,359.

Year 12, their S&P 500 = $6,620,359 x 1.10 - $80,000 = $7,202,394.

Year 13, their S&P 500 = $7,202,394 x 1.10 - $80,000 = $7,842,634.

Year 14, their S&P 500 = $7,842,634 x 1.10 - $80,000 = $8,546,897.

Year 15, their S&P 500 = $8,546,897 x 1.10 - $80,000 = $9,321,587.

Year 16, their S&P 500 = $9,321,587 x 1.10 - $80,000 = $10,173,746.

Year 17, their S&P 500 = $10,173,746 x 1.10 - $80,000 = $11,111,120.

Year 18, their S&P 500 = $11,111,120 x 1.10 - $80,000 = $12,142,232.

Year 19, their S&P 500 = $12,142,232 x 1.10 - $80,000 = $13,276,456.

Year 20, their S&P 500 = $13,276,456 x 1.10 - $80,000 = $14,524,102.

At age 70, their total amount = $160,000 + $14,524,102 = $14,684,102.

Important Point. By using the money tree method of this chapter, their wealth grows nicely from $3 million to more than $14 million. This is even when they do not work, consume $80,000 per year, and use a simple, passive investing method.

Now, let's compare this money tree result with the myths.

3. Myth 1 - Move Money into CD when You Retire

Betty and Bob listen to the teaching of "playing it safe", and want to use the CD method. In year 2020, the one-year CD returns about 0.27%, and the five-year CD returns 0.43% percent. In the past 20 years, the CD rates have averaged about 2-3%. To cut the CD method some slack, let's use a high-end CD rate of 3% for the calculation.

In year 0, Betty and Bob put $3,000,000 into a CD that returns 3% annually. Every year, it increases by 3%. Every year, they sell $80,000 to pay for their living expenses.

The detailed calculation is included in Appendix 1 at the end of this book. Using the CD method, at age 70, their wealth amount = $3,268,704.

4. Myth 2 - Move Money into Bonds when You Retire

Cindy and Carl choose to invest in bond funds. Bond mutual return approximately 4-6%. To cut the bonds method some slack, let's use the high-end of 6% in the calculation.

In year 0, Cindy and Carl put $3,000,000 into a bond mutual fund that returns 6% annually. Every year, they sell $80,000 to pay for their living expenses.

The detailed calculation is shown in Appendix 2 at the end of this book. Using the bonds method, at age 70, their wealth amount = $6,678,559.

5. Myth 3 - Use a Mixture of Stocks and Bonds

Conventional wisdom suggests a mixture of stocks and bonds for retirees. The ratio of stocks to bonds depend on the person's age, risk tolerance factor, etc. In addition, typically, the suggestion is that the person should rebalance the stock-to-bond ratio each year to reflect the aging. The suggested stock-to-bond ratios for retirees range from 50/50, to 40% stocks/60% bonds, to 30% stocks/70% bonds, to 100% bonds for older seniors and those who choose to be more conservative.

Debbie and Doug retire at the age of 50 with $3 million. They want to use the stocks/bonds mixture method. They choose 40% stocks and 60% bonds, which is an intermediate ratio among the aforementioned ratios.

Assume that they select six good mutual funds that return 8% annually for the next 15 years (there are plenty of mutual funds that do worse than this). Bond mutual funds historically return about 4-6% annually. To cut this method some slack, assume 6% return in the following estimate.

The following simple estimate does not require Debbie

207

and Doug to rebalance by selling some mutual funds and putting it into bonds each year, which will reduce their return because in this example, mutual funds returns 8%, and bonds return 6%. A strict mixture would mandate them to rebalance each year as they age, to reduce the stocks percentage and increase the bonds percentage each year. This is quite troublesome to a lot of retirees.

Alternatively, if they choose a special type of mutual funds that perform this annual rebalancing action for them, then their mutual fund fees go up. As we have already discussed, this can diminish their return. Therefore, no rebalancing is included in the following simple illustration.

In year 0, Debbie and Doug have $1,800,000 in bonds, and $1,200,000 in mutual funds.

Every year, they sell $80,000 of their bonds to pay for their living expenses. The detailed calculation is shown in Appendix 3 at the end of this book.

In year # 20, their bonds = $2,829,998 (Appendix 3).

Their mutual funds grow in 20 years to: $1,200,000 x 1.08**20 = $5,593,149.

At age 70, their wealth amount = $2,829,998 + $5,593,149 = $8,423,147.

6. Notes for the Calculations

(1) This chapter assumes $3 million at age 50, to illustrate the point. You may follow the aforementioned

procedures using your own actual numbers. For example, you may use $1 million at age 45. Or $6 million at age 56, etc. You will reach the same conclusion that the money tree method grows much more money for you than the popular myths.

(2) These simple estimates avoid making the calculations too complicated to risk losing the readers. For example, to pay for living expenses, the $80,000 investment is sold once a year. In reality, you will likely sell a fixed amount each month for dollar cost averaging.

(3) This chapter uses $80,000 for the annual living expenses, because the national median family income for the United States for FY 2019 was $75,500. However, some areas are more expensive than others. You can repeat the estimates by using a living expense number that is suitable for your own situation. Maybe you need only $60,000 per year for living expenses, or maybe you need $100,000 or $150,000. Just make sure that you use the same living expense number to compare the myths with the money tree method. This will not change the results that the money tree method grows much more wealth for you in your retirement than the myths.

(4) In the simple calculation, the living expenses number is not increased each year to account for inflation. You may increase the selling by 2% each year to increase your living expenses number to offset the inflation. This chapter omits the 2% inflation for living expenses to keep the math simple. In addition, the 2% inflation can be offset by the following reasons.

For many people, when they retire, they sell their bigger

house and buy a smaller house. This difference will help them supplement their retirement, which would be more than enough to offset the inflation.

Some retirees move from an expensive neighborhood in the west coast or east coast, to a less expensive southern area. The differences in housing values could give them extra funds for retirement. In addition, they may decide to start withdrawing from their social security to supplement for their retirement.

These factors are more than enough to offset the inflation. However, if you still want to include the inflation, just add 2% into the living expenses each year in the above math. You will reach the same result that the money tree method grows multimillions of dollars more for you than the myths.

(5) For the calculation using the S&P 500, I did not use the S&P 500 rate of return for the last ten years which was 14.3%. I use an average return of 10%, based on the return of 1965-2020. If you choose other funds to invest in, make sure that you use the long-term average return, not just that of only one decade. This will avoid overestimating the rate of return.

(6) For those of you who worry: "What if the S&P 500 crashes?" If the S&P 500 booms, you sell $80,000 each year to keep two years of living expenses in cash. If the S&P 500 crashes, you do the same. If you retire at, say, 50 years of age and live till, say, 80, that is 30 years. For the 30-year average, the S&P 500 will likely revert to its historic 10% per year.

Therefore, just ignore the bumps in the S&P 500, be emotionally detached, and enjoy your retirement.

(7) For those of you who may say that "the money tree method grows my wealth to $14 million but I do not need so much money," please think this way. If you live a relaxed life without paying attention to the market's ups and downs, if you have financial freedom and don't worry about money, and if you help others and live a happy and satisfying life, chances are that you likely will live well past 80 years of age.

With advances in medicine, many people will live into their 80s and 90s. The money tree method will enable you to have no worry about money and retain your ability to give back.

7. The Importance of a Simple Choice

By choosing the money tree method in the example of Amy and Adam, we can make $6 million to $11 million more than the conventional wisdom methods. In addition, the money tree method is simple, easy, and effortless.

Furthermore, the estimate above is from age 50 to 70 only. If we hold our investments for 5 more years, the difference will be even much bigger than what is shown in the chart.

Your life is a result of the choices you make. We choose where to go to college and what to study. We choose a career to pursue. We choose whom to marry to and when to start a family. We choose whether to sit in the couch watching TV or getting up to exercise.

By choosing the money tree method, we will have millions of dollars more for ourselves and our loved ones.

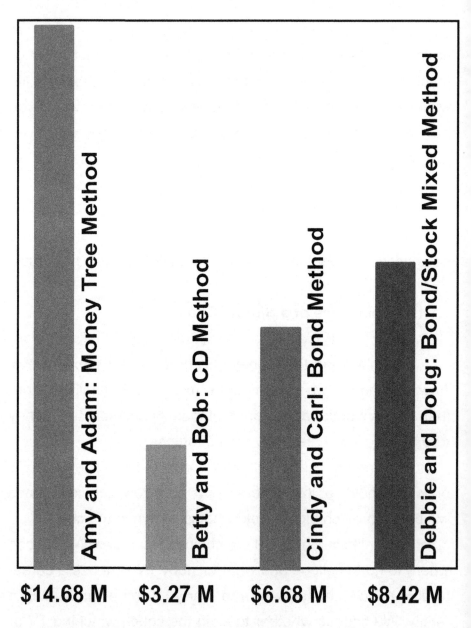

$14.68 M   **$3.27 M**   **$6.68 M**   **$8.42 M**

    With increasing life expectancy and continuous breakthroughs in medical science and biotechnology, many people will living well into their 80s and 90s in the future. The innovative and unorthodox money tree method of "two years of living expenses in cash, all else in the S&P 500" will continue to grow substantial wealth for you and your loved ones.

You may ask: "Why do I need millions of dollars at the age of 70? I don't need that much money when I am old, so I don't care which method to use." Well, as President Ronald Reagan said: "Money can't buy happiness, but it will certainly get you a better class of memories." The additional millions from the simple money tree method will increase your quality of life and create better retirement memories. Furthermore, these extra millions will get your loved ones a better class of memories too.

In addition, please note the following reasons.

(1) Don't be surprised by the big money numbers because they will have less purchasing power 30 to 40 years from now.

(2) Due to increased life expectancy, you and your loved ones will likely live longer with ensuing expenses to cover.

(3) Medical bills are expensive.

(4) With the money tree method growing substantial extra money for you, you can provide for your loved ones and for charitable causes to help others.

By making a simple choice for the money tree method, you change your life and the lives of your loved ones.

If you want to get outside of the box, you have to think

outside of the box. Don't be boxed in by the conventional wisdom and financial myths. If you want to be among the small minority group of self-made millionaires, you have to avoid following the crowd and the conventional wisdom that have kept ordinary people average. If you want to be financially outstanding, you have to stand out and stand alone in your financial practices. This is the purpose of the innovative, unorthodox, and box-busting money tree methods.

8. A Simple, Yet Powerful, Money Tree to Grow Millions

Besides growing millions for you, another merit of the money tree method is that it is very simple to understand:

Two years of living expenses in cash, all other investments in the S&P 500.

This is easy to execute. It takes only a few minutes per year to execute this method. You do not have to calculate ratios and percentages and try to rebalance a dozen mutual funds and bonds each year.

The money tree method is simple. It does not require you to research on the quarterly reports of companies to pick stocks. It does not require you to keep up with the news and financial reports. It does not require you to deal with rental properties. All you do is to keep two years of living expenses in cash in the bank, and keep the rest in the S&P 500. You can be on the beach, in a mountain, partying with friends, spending time with relatives, or living in another country.

Albert Einstein ranked the level of intelligence as:

1. Smart;

2. Intelligent;

3. Genius;

4. Simple.

"Simple" is considered the highest level of intelligence. This was manifested in his simple but powerful formula: $E = mc^{**}2$.

The money tree method is simple, powerful, and lucrative. It will continue to grow millions well into your retirement for you and your loved ones to enjoy life, to have financial freedom, and to give and help others.

Wishing you a long, enjoyable, highly profitable and satisfying retirement!

The preceding chapters have demonstrated simple and highly profitable money tree methods for college students, young professionals, home owners, 401k and mutual fund investors, small real estate investors, middle-aged employees, 50-year olds, and retirees.

Using an analogy to sports, the preceding chapters have focused on building up the physical strength and technical skills. A champion athlete has (1) physical strength, (2) technical skills, and (3) inner emotional strength.

The next two chapters focus on the inner emotional strength for the investor. They makes this book complete.

Chapter 21. The Eagle's Two Wings: Courage and Caution

Myth: **Fearless.**

Money Tree: **Balance.**

I hope this book and my personal real-life examples will inspire people to learn to invest and achieve financial freedom. However, my experiences and conversations with many others have revealed two common obstacles blocking our way to financial freedom. This book would not be complete without providing effective methods to overcome these obstacles.

One is lack of courage, which I will address in this chapter. The other obstacle is the emotional stress of investing, which is addressed in the next chapter.

A lack of courage is common in investing, when people are faced with moving large sums of their hard-earned money. People often fear failure. This fear leads people to be overly cautious and conservative in investing, thus losing the opportunity to making millions along the way.

1. Balance Beam Gymnastics

Simone Biles is one of the best gymnasts of all time. She has so far won a total of thirty Olympic and World Championship medals, thus becoming the most decorated gymnast in the history of the United States. Among all her achievements, she is a three-time World balance beam champion. Her stunning moves on the balance beam are truly amazing and a pure joy to watch.

On the balance beam, one step left, you fall. One step right, you fall.

In investing, one must also maintain a balance between caution and courage. One step left (caution without courage), you fall. One step right (courage without caution), you fall.

On the one hand, the small investor needs to have courage. If s/he keeps thinking that the sky is falling, then s/he will be too scared to pull the trigger to invest. If s/he keeps thinking that the stock market is going to crash and the housing market is going to crash, then s/he will be too worried to invest, thereby missing good opportunities to grow wealth and achieve financial freedom. This will actually put him or her in a more risky situation lacking financial freedom.

However, rational caution, careful analyses and due diligence are indeed needed. Without them, an investor can go broke and be wiped out.

Here are examples of the cautions that I exercise:

Do not over leverage;

Know my circle of competence;

Know the boundary of my circle of competence and stay strictly inside;

When buying real estate, stay in my own neighborhood;

Do not enter into unfamiliar markets;

Do not enter into businesses that I don't understand;

Do not enter into deals that are too complicated;

If the trend is unfavorable, stay away;

If the math does not show a sure and significant win, and if there is doubt, walk away. There are always more opportunities than my amount of money.

These safeguards have served me well. As long as you follow a checklist of safeguards, you have the "caution" part covered, and you just need the courage to take action. You can memorize the checklist, but you still need courage to take action. As the Spanish writer Baltasar Gracián observed:

"Without courage, wisdom bears no fruit."[1]

2. Watch for Signs of Over-Heating and Bubbles

For example, buying a house in 2006-2007 would see a price crash by 1/3 nationwide in average by 2012. Prior to the crash, housing prices were increasing by double digits, such as 15% per year, for several years in a row. During the boom years, I knew two computer engineers who quit their jobs to

218

become real estate agents. When a builder opened a new neighborhood development not far from where I lived, people lined up and camped out overnight in order to grab a lot to have a new house built. These were "bubble" signs. Therefore, if you see signs of overheat such as hot bidding wars, be careful.

For me, if the housing price appreciation in the past several years has been similar to the long-term historic average, I would feel comfortable. If the past several years have had much higher appreciations, then I would not buy, because the next several years may stagnate or decline, for the price to gradually revert to the long-term average.

Assume that your neighborhood has had a long-term housing value appreciation of 4% in the past twenty years. Assume that your neighborhood saw 7% appreciation in 2019 and 10% in 2020. When you decide whether to buy a rental house or not, you should use the 4% appreciation to estimate your rate of return, not the 7% or 10%.

I know an investor who was buying apartment buildings in a big city near me in 2018 and 2019, and kindly invited me to join him. His calculations, based on the past 7-8 years, showed excellent return in the future. I declined, knowing that prices for apartment buildings in that big city had gone up extraordinarily well for 7-8 years already. These things usually will eventually revert to the long-term historic average. Over-heating will be followed by a cooling period. Something will happen to trigger the decline and cooling. This time, it was Covid-19. Now, at the end of 2020, apartment building vacancies in that big city have shot up and rents have dropped by 20-30%.

3. Annual Dollar Cost Averaging to Buy Rental Properties

If my local real estate market has been going up significantly faster than the historic average for several years, that would trigger my caution. I would wait and not buy.

However, crashes do not happen often. The 2008-2009 housing crash was referred to as a once-in-a-lifetime event. If I keep waiting for a crash, I would miss investment opportunities. Most of the time, the market goes up in a rather normal fashion.

Yet, I understand that some people still worry that the housing market will crash. The following is a simple dollar-cost-averaging illustration on how to control such a risk.

Jeannie and her husband bought a rental house in 2007. They were unlucky and the markets tanked. However, they kept saving for the down payment and bought another house in 2009. Then another house in 2011. Then another house in 2013, etc. They continued, and their rents gradually increased, giving them more cash flow. Housing price appreciated. Their mortgages are being paid down. Their wealth has been growing nicely. They retired in 2020.

Therefore, even if their timing was off, they mitigated their risk via dollar cost averaging. While the term "dollar cost averaging" usually refers to the investment of a certain amount of money into the stock market every month, we can use the same concept to buy a rental property every year and keep doing it for a decade. Instead of the monthly dollar cost averaging, buying a house every year could be called annual dollar cost averaging.

I know several people who just kept buying houses as rental properties year after year after year. Those who are persistent, who buy a house very year and continue to do that for a decade, are eventually rewarded with financial freedom.

Every decade, there are people persistently investing year after year who achieve financial freedom. Every decade, there are others who worry and wait, and miss good opportunities.

4. Dollar Cost Averaging for Equity Index Funds

If one prefers to invest in an index fund such as the S&P 500 and not in rental properties, or would like to invest in both, the same method applies to growing wealth while minimizing the risk: Dollar cost averaging, and holding for the long term.

For example, some people worry that the stock market will crash and they do not dare to invest. As Peter Lynch observed:

"More people lost money waiting for corrections and anticipating corrections than the actual corrections."[2]

The following is a simple illustration on how to mitigate such a risk.

Ridley started to invest in the S&P 500. He got unlucky because he started in the year 2000. He put in $10,000 into the

S&P 500 in 2000, but then the market crashed in 2000 and 2001.

However, Ridley had the courage to tell himself: "I'm not going to pay attention to the short-term ups and downs. I will keep investing and do dollar cost averaging."

In 2001, Ridley put another $10,000 into the S&P 500. In 2002, he put in another $10,000. In 2003, he put in another $10,000.

His salary increased; he started to put in $20,000 into the S&P 500 annually. After a few more years, he started to put in $30,000 into the S&P 500 per year.

Ridley kept doing this for two decades.

How time flies. Now it is 2020. Ridley looks at his S&P 500 account, and it has done very well. He smiles. His wealth has grown nicely. He decides to retire.

As Maya Angelou said: "Courage is the most important of all the virtues because without courage, you can't practice any other virtue consistently."[3]

Indeed, it takes courage to take action to invest when faced with volatility. With possibilities of crashes, it takes courage to be patient, be persistent, and thereby reach financial freedom.

5. Courage

I am not a courageous person. I worry a lot. Most of the things that I worry about do not actually happen.

In Example 3 in Chapter 1, my wife and I borrowed money from three lenders and poured that cash into the S&P 500. The difficulty was the short term. The market is unpredictable in the short term. It may decline next week. It may crash next month. That is why it takes courage.

For the eagle to fly, the two wings are balanced to work together. An investor also needs two wings: Courage and caution.

When I did the clicks on my computer to put the money into the S&P 500, I was nervous. What if it drops by 10% next week? I reminded myself to focus on the long term, which helped mitigate my fear. I looked at the S&P 500 return table from 1965-2019, showing an average of 10% per year. I re-read my own writing on positive carry. If I borrow money from Peter at an interest rate of 3.5%, and give it to John who pays me 10% return, I should be fine in the long term, even if the long-term return is only 8% and not 10%. I told myself to block out and ignore the fear about short-term drops.

What if the S&P 500 crashes in 2021? I will try to do more cash-out refinances to put more money into the S&P 500.

What if the S&P 500 crashes in 2022? I will try to do more cash-out refinances to put more money into the S&P 500.

As Roman historian Publius Tacitus said: "The desire for safety stands against every great and noble enterprise."[4]

Focusing on the long term and planning to do annual dollar cost averaging helped remove my fear and give me more courage.

The reward for my tiny courage to invest in the S&P 500 in year 2020 was $0.283 million in net profit. This was using borrowed money from three lenders, with 0 money out of our pocket. Therefore, one could say that:

The rate of return = net profit/money out of our pocket = $0.283 million/0 = infinite.

With real estate, my wife and I bought townhouses as rental properties in our neighborhood. The math showed rates of return above 20%, sometimes at 30% to 40%. Our local market appreciated at about 4% annually from 2011-2019. There was no over-heating. The schools are excellent and the job market is relatively stable. These facts gave us the courage to make the purchases.

Courage is not blind. Courage is knowing the market, doing the due diligence, seeing that the math makes sense, and focusing on the long-term reward.

In addition, I overcame my fear through reading investment books and the stories of successful investors. Similarly, by reading this book, I hope it will give your courage. Knowledge and experience will give you confidence, grow your investing capabilities, and increase your wealth.

Chapter 22. No Pain, Much Gain

Myth: **No pain, no gain.**

Money Tree: **No pain, much gain. Staying calm, joyful and thankful enhances wealth growth.**

1. Pain, No Gain

Another obstacle that blocks the way toward financial freedom is the emotional pain and stress of investing.

A friend, who is an experienced investor in one of the inventing groups with me, shared recently:

"I did research on this stock, analyzed the future of the industry, read about the founder and the leadership team, and estimated its intrinsic value. My due diligence showed that this would be a 10-bagger. I bought it at about $30/share. After two months, it increased to $50/share. Then it started to become very volatile. Then over a period of a couple of months, it decreased to $10/share. That period of time was very painful to me. As the stock price crashed, my faith in this stock and in my analysis also crashed. I was kicking myself for not selling at $50."

"Eventually, the stock price gradually rebounded to over $30, and I quickly sold, above breakeven with a small profit. Now, the stock price is at $127, and I have been kicking myself again for selling too early."

The anxiety and pain on investing prompted this friend to sell and miss the subsequent surge. Therefore, "pain" leads to "no gain."

Another friend shared this story:

"My husband bought a bunch of shares of this stock, after reading many articles. However, after he bought it, it started a downward trend. Eventually, it went down by about 25%. It was painful to watch. We waited patiently. Finally, after suffering for nearly three months, the share price went back to the breakeven point, and I sold all his shares with a sigh of relief. But now, the price has just doubled, and I have lost $90,000 in profit for selling too early. I missed the big jump and lost $90,000 in profit."

Even if a small investor was smart enough and lucky enough to buy Apple stocks in the 1990s, how many people can hold it for nearly three decades? Apple has crashed by over 75% multiple times. Its worst crash was by 82%. How many people can stand the pain of watching their account losing 75% or 82% of their money? Most people would have sold at the wrong time, and possibly been scarred for life.

In the stock market, the emotional stress and anxiety

that the investor feels can prompt the investor to stop investing, or sell in panic at the wrong time, thereby missing the profits and opportunities.

Anxiety and stress can also do damage in real estate investing. I know some new landlords who quit after a year or two. The tenant did not take care of the house. The yard was messy, the house was dirty. The kids drew on the walls. The dog peed on the carpet. The new landlord suffers anxiety and emotional pain. After the tenant leaves, the new landlord sells the house and washes his hands of the mess.

In doing so, the landlord misses the opportunity to harvest 20-30% annual returns in future years and decades. And more importantly, they miss the opportunity to buy more rental properties and achieve financial freedom.

The emotional anxiety of investing can make the investor lose millions and can kill the financial freedom. Indeed, this can amount to one of the biggest financial costs in life.

This means: Pain, no gain.

How should we manager, minimize and avoid the anxiety and pain of investing?

That is the purpose of this chapter.

2. No Pain, Much Gain

People say: "No pain, no gain."

In investing, I like to say: "Pain, no gain. No pain, much gain."

This means that I like to minimize and avoid the emotional pain of investing, thereby to be able to calmly analyze, to seize the opportunities and stay the course, in order to harvest the gains.

If I can avoid the pain in investing, then I can stay rational, focus on the math, and avoid making regrettable decisions while in anxiety. Without the pain, and with a clear and rational mind, we can invest intelligently and achieve financial freedom.

Therefore, "no pain, much gain."

My son Darnell graduated from college and has been working for a big company. Due to Covid-19, he has been working from home. He is healthy and strong, and has been lifting weights in the family gym. In November 2020, he needed to have a small surgery done on two of his toes. I drove him to a medical center where the surgery was performed.

Of course, as a scaredy-cat, I did not dare to watch the small surgery. It took less than half an hour. Once Darnell was back in the car, he briefly described how it went.

First, the doctor rubbed Darnell's toes with a numbing gel. After a couple of minutes, the doctor injected local anesthesia. Then he did the surgery. Darnell did not feel much pain at all. Once home, Darnell also took Motrin every six hours for three days. He recovered quickly, and started lifting weights three days later.

To summarize this experience: To gain physical health in Darnell's toes through a small surgery, the medical treatment to minimize the pain involved (1) numbing gel, (2) local anesthesia, and (3) Motrin.

Similarly, to gain financial health through investing, the following describes the medicaments to minimize the emotional stress and anxiety, thereby enabling the investor to earn the largest possible gains.

3. Numbing Gel: Do Not Think About It or Look at It Often

I try to desensitize my feelings and emotions in investing by keeping some distance from my investments. I do not think about or look at my investments often.

For example, for my 401k, money is being deducted from my paychecks every two weeks and invested into an SP 500 index fund. Whether the market crashes or makes a new high, the biweekly investing continues automatically, without me doing anything. I look at my 401k account only once a year, at the end of the year when my wife and we tally our total wealth. Other than that, I do not look at it or think about it. I do not second guess, thinking:

"Wow, the market is crazily high. It is so expensive now. Will it crash soon? Should I sell and move the money to a money market account?"

Or: "Oops, the market crashed today. Will it go down further? Should I move my 401k to a bond fund?"

By avoiding to look at or think about it, I do not feel the stress. In addition, it saves me time.

Furthermore, statistically, people who stay the course do better than those who try to time the market and move their money in and out of the market.

For my regular account which is 100% invested in the S&P 500, I look at the account only when I need to buy more. Even at those times, I limit myself to only a couple of minutes to perform the clicks on my computer to put the money into the S&P 500. Then I log out.

So, I keep some emotional distance from my S&P 500 investing. This provides emotional detachment and avoids stress and anxiety. And the results have been quite satisfactory. The S&P 500 in the long term beats most mutual funds and hedge funds.

4. Local Anesthesia: Minimize My Sensitivity to Details and Avoid Being Buried in Details

For our rental properties, I rely on a team. I use other people's time and talents, pay them well, and treat them with respect. They can do things that I cannot do. They have talents and skills that I do not possess.

This reduces my stress. This helps me to stay out of the details such as damages, messiness, toilets, trees growing too big, etc. This helps me to stay above the noise and avoid getting bogged down by negative issues. I get technical, time and emotional support from my team to avoid getting burned out. This has helped me focus on the big picture, buy more properties, and grow the "pie" bigger.

For example, in November 2020, a tenant's heating was not working. I texted my real estate agent, who recommended a good contractor. I texted the contractor, and he went to the tenant's townhouse. After inspection, he called me and suggested replacing the HVAC system as it was 17 years old and not worth repairing. I told him to go ahead. He replaced it with a new system and I mailed him a check. My time: about 15 minutes.

Another example: a tenant's oven was not working. I texted my long-time handyman, who went and found that he couldn't fix it, but knew a good contractor who could. I told him: "You have my full trust. Please do whatever it takes using your judgment." My handyman monitored the whole process and I only needed to make the payment. Relying on a team helps take my anxiety and nervousness away.

These methods help take my anxiety away. To help you remember, think about the analogy of the local anesthesia for Darnell's toes that took the physical pain away and made him feel comfortable and at peace.

5. Retaking Motrin When Needed: Revisit the Analysis, Math and Books

In investing, there are many times when you have happy harvests and pleasant gains.

However, there are also times of challenges, setbacks,

ups and downs, and difficulties.

The doctor told Darnell to take some Motrin every six houses when needed. If the pain recurs, the patient takes the painkiller again.

Similarly, when an investor is in financial and emotional pain, he or she could take "painkillers" when needed. Retaking the painkiller means revisiting the math that made sense to reassure yourself and soothe your anxiety. It means revisiting the due diligence and analyses.

For example, for a rental house, perhaps a major repair killed the cash flow. Instead of feeling emotional pain, it helps to revisit the math (such as Chapter 14) that shows that even with 0 cash flow, the rate of return was still, say, 21%.

Or, maybe the tenant was laid off due to Covid-19 and missed several months of rent payments, and the net cash flow for the year became negative. Instead of suffering from the pain, revisit the math that showed that the rate of return could still be, say, 18%. That still easily beats the 10% for the S&P 500 and 14% for Mr. Buffett in the past quarter century. Looking at the 18% annual return helps take the pain away.

Putting money in a "painless safe harbor" cannot make annual returns such as 18% or 27% to achieve financial freedom. The "painless safe harbor" would actually be more painful financially due to the missed opportunities to grow wealth.

I remind myself the quote of William Shedd: "A ship is safe in harbor, but that's not what ships are for."[1]

My money is safe in a CD earning 1%, but that's not what money trees are for. (Please note that CD rates and interest rates change with time.)

With storms, wind, rain and sunshine, trees grow bigger and stronger. By managing and minimizing the risks intelligently, money trees grow bigger and more fruitful.

Furthermore, even if there was a major setback in a year, it helps to keep the long-term perspective. Revisit your math to remind yourself that in the long term of a decade or two, your total return will still be excellent.

For Darnell's toes, in the three days after his surgery, when the moderate physical pain recurred, he took Motrin again, following the doctor's instructions.

In our investing journey, when emotional anxiety recurs, revisit the analyses.

In addition, you may reread a few book chapters that had given you wisdom, strength and courage in the past, and would also help take away your current pain.

6. My Other Weapons to Kill Emotional Anxiety of Investing

Use the Money Tree Methods to Obtain a High Rate of Return. In investing, unexpected things happen. Covid-19 hits and a tenant misses rent payments. The HVAC fails in the summer and costs $5,000 to be replaced. If your rate of return is just 10%, and then these setbacks knock it down by a few points to 7%, that can hurt.

However, if your rate of return is 25% and these setbacks knock it down by a few points to 22%, you do not feel as bad. This is because you know that your 22% still far exceeds the 10% long-term return of the S&P 500.

As shown in the beginning of this book, our wealth growth rate averaged 27.2% annually from 2011-2020. This was due to the use of leverage, with safeguards. The rate of return would have been much lower without leverage.

Furthermore, even when we invested in the S&P 500, we borrowed money from the lenders to do it (Chapter 1). We used no money out of our own pocket; hence, our own invested capital amount was 0. Therefore, the rate of return (net profit divided by 0) could be considered infinite. These methods help increase our rate of return. Then, if we are hit with some setbacks that reduce our return, say, from 27% to 22%, it is still a good return. The money tree methods help minimize the possible setbacks and anxiety of investing.

Being Prepared Helps Minimize the Anxiety of Investing. For example, with our investing in the S&P 500 using borrowed money (Chapter 1), what if the S&P 500 crashes? That could cause significant emotional pain.

The market was expensive at the end of 2020, and this may bring back the memory of 1999. Will the market continue to make new highs, or will it crash? I do not know. I control the risks by dollar cost averaging, holding it for the long term, and preparing more capital to invest if the market crashes. My wife and I use two methods to be prepared. (1) We plan to do cash-out refinances every year, or every couple of years, to put more money into the S&P 500. If it crashes in 2021, we plan to put more money into it, which means that we would be buying low. If it crashes in 2022, we plan to put more money into it, and so on. (2) In 2020, we used a commercial line of credit and a HELOC to borrow money to invest in the S&P 500. We started in April and stopped buying in October. In November and December 2020, we used our cash flow to pay back the commercial line of credit and the HELOC. In two months, we paid back $150,000. We plan to continue to use the cash flow to pay down the lines of credit in the coming months, to make the lines of credit available again for our future borrowing. In this way, we are prepared with more funds to buy low, in case there is a crash in the future. Being prepared helps take away the anxiety and fear of a possible crash, and to seize future investment opportunities.

Exercise. I have found that regular exercise helps me to keep going in my investing journey. I walk and jog, totaling about 20,000 steps daily. In addition, I do some pushups and sit-ups. Exercise helps me to clear my mind and maintain a positive mood. It trains my perseverance, endurance, patience, and self-discipline, traits that are important in investing too.

Jokes. I like to read and tell jokes and funny stories. I like to make people laugh. My kids call me "the jokester". This helps distract me from the stresses of life. It is beneficial for an investor to have a good sense of humor, and to laugh and make others laugh. This provides an effective painkiller in life and in investing.

If you are faced with some challenges and do not feel like laughing, read some jokes and funny stories and laugh. It has health benefits as well as investing benefits.

Remember, high stress and anxiety are a carcinogen.

I hope this chapter helps minimize your emotional anxiety in investing. Indeed, too many people quit in real estate investing after a year or two, due to such anxiety. Too many people sell their stocks and mutual funds at the wrong time, at the market bottom, due to such anxiety.

Emotional pain in investing can kill financial freedom.

Count My Blessings. If the stock market drops by 30%, like it did in March 2020, or if a tenant cannot pay rent, it helps to count my blessings. Many immigrants have wonderful stories about them coming to the Unites States with only $100 in their pockets, and eventually realizing their amazing American dreams. This is a great country, the home of the innovative, and the land of opportunity.

In 1988, I came to America with negative $2,000, because I had to borrow money for my wedding in China and to buy the airplane ticket. Since then, my wife and I have received blessings far more than we could have imagined back in the 1980s.

I tell my kids: "Let's all be grateful. If mom and I had stayed in China and had not come to America, we would have had only one child. Then we would not have had Darnell and Joyce."

Our children Sweetie, Moutai, Darnell and Joyce exercising. Being grateful is good for health and for investing. Our kids know that if my wife and I had not come to America, we would have had only one child.

Counting our blessings helps me to have perspective. It helps me to be a grateful person. It lifts me up above the small details. It strengthens me to weather challenges and setbacks. While counting my blessings, I do not sweat the small stuff. I focus on the entire pie, not a small missing slice. This helps us grow a bigger pie. This helps take away the investing anxiety.

Help Others. My rental houses are located in an excellent school district, and most of my tenants have been paying rents without issues. A couple of them have had difficulties paying the rent from time to time. My wife and I try to be kind and help them, and give them more time to work things out. In a couple of cases, we lowered the rent and waived late fees to help them out.

Some books teach the readers to run the rentals as a business, not as a charity. They are right. My personal experience, though, is that having a charitable heart helps me to help tenants, minimizes my emotional anxiety, avoids negative thoughts and burnout, and gives me more strength to grow the rental portfolio bigger.

I also try to assist others who aspire to become successful investors. For example, my first book *$5 Million in 8 Years: Real Estate Investing on the Side* helped a couple in Pennsylvania. The wife always wanted to invest in real estate, but the husband did not want to; my book helped unite them to pursue their investing and financial freedom together. The same happened to another couple, except that in this case, the husband wanted to buy rental properties but the wife did not want to. And my book helped unite them in their pursuit. A friend in Virginia read my book and decided to go into real estate. She took the exam for the real estate agent license. With the plan to buy a rental house every year and persist for a decade, she will reach her dream of financial freedom.

Discussing with them and sharing my experience with them help me to be a stronger investor. This is similar to the case where the teachers need to be strong for their students, and the parents need to be strong for their kids. Sharing my experience and assisting others to succeed reminds me to be strong for their sake. It reminds me to be calm when facing challenges. It reminds me to focus on the big picture of growing wealth, and not get bogged down by some messy and negative issues, in order to set a good example.

By helping others to have courage to invest, it helps myself to be more courageous.

As Amelia Earhart said: "Courage is the price that life exacts for granting peace. The soul that knows it not, knows no release from little things."[2]

Courage leads to peace. Courage helps remove anxiety in investing and brings peace to the mind.

Courage in investing helps secure financial freedom, bringing financial peace to you and your loved ones.

By helping others, it gives me greater strength and drive to do better and to further grow our family's wealth.

Therefore, give back and help make others financially healthier and wealthier. This, in return, will also make us wealthier and happier.

This would be a melodious and harmonious note for this book to end on.

Happy and successful investing!

Acknowledgement

I thank my parents for their hard work, sacrifice and love. They lived through famine and poverty, demonstrating unimaginable resilience and endurance. When China finally opened its door to the world, my parents resisted the temptation to send us to work and make quick money, and instead, invested in our education and sent all three kids to college. Their wisdom and sacrifice have changed the lives of me and my two brothers.

I am grateful to my wife for her love, encouragement and traveling the journey of life with me. I thank our three kids S, D and J and son-in-law M who are intelligent, wise, responsible, generous, loving, and decent. S, D and J helped revising, polishing and publishing this book. I am grateful to my parents-in-law for their love and support. My gratitude also goes to my brothers and their families for their love and support. I love you all.

I thank Long W for his tremendous help; I could not have done this without you. My special thanks go to Lyle K, Bonita K, and Ken K for their kindness, generosity and advice. My gratitude also goes to Zhen C, Brian L, Francis and Clara C, Dwayne A, Larry C and Carl S, for their kind support and generous help. I am grateful to YF, Sherry, Nancy, Jon, and Duncan for all their great help. I also thank WW, HL, YZ and XM for their support. Thank you all so much!

Appendix 1 for Chapter 20

Year 0, Betty and Bob put $3,000,000 into a CD that returns 3% annually. Every year, it increases by 3%. Every year, they sell $80,000 for living expenses.

Year 1, $3,000,000 x 1.03 - $80,000 = $3,010,000

Year 2, $3,010,000 x 1.03 - $80,000 = $3,020,300

Year 3, $3,020,300 x 1.03 - $80,000 = $3,030,909

Year 4, $3,030,909 x 1.03 - $80,000 = $3,041,836

Year 5, $3,041,836 x 1.03 - $80,000 = $3,053,091

Year 6, $3,053,091 x 1.03 - $80,000 = $3,064,684

Year 7, $3,064,684 x 1.03 - $80,000 = $3,076,625

Year 8, $3,076,625 x 1.03 - $80,000 = $3,088,923

Year 9, $3,088,923 x 1.03 - $80,000 = $3,101,591

Year 10, $3,101,591 x 1.03 - $80,000 = $3,114,639

Year 11, $3,114,639 x 1.03 - $80,000 = $3,128,078

Year 12, $3,128,078 x 1.03 - $80,000 = $3,141,920

Year 13, $3,141,920 x 1.03 - $80,000 = $3,156,178

Year 14, $3,156,178 x 1.03 - $80,000 = $3,170,863

Year 15, $3,170,863 x 1.03 - $80,000 = $3,185,989

Year 16, $3,185,989 x 1.03 - $80,000 = $3,201,569

Year 17, $3,201,569 x 1.03 - $80,000 = $3,217,616

Year 18, $3,217,616 x 1.03 - $80,000 = $3,234,144

Year 19, $3,234,144 x 1.03 - $80,000 = $3,251,169

Year 20, $3,251,169 x 1.03 - $80,000 = $3,268,704

Appendix 2 for Chapter 20

Year 0, Cindy and Carl put $3,000,000 into a bond mutual fund that returns 6% annually. Every year, they sell $80,000 for living expenses.

Year 1, $3,000,000 x 1.06 - $80,000 = $3,100,000

Year 2, $3,100,000 x 1.06 - $80,000 = $3,206,000

Year 3, $3,206,000 x 1.06 - $80,000 = $3,318,360

Year 4, $3,318,360 x 1.06 - $80,000 = $3,437,462

Year 5, $3,437,462 x 1.06 - $80,000 = $3,563,709

Year 6, $3,563,709 x 1.06 - $80,000 = $3,697,532

Year 7, $3,697,532 x 1.06 - $80,000 = $3,839,384

Year 8, $3,839,384 x 1.06 - $80,000 = $3,989,747

Year 9, $3,989,747 x 1.06 - $80,000 = $4,149,132

Year 10, $4,149,132 x 1.06 - $80,000 = $4,318,079

Year 11, $4,318,079 x 1.06 - $80,000 = $4,497,164

Year 12, $4,497,164 x 1.06 - $80,000 = $4,686,994

Year 13, $4,686,994 x 1.06 - $80,000 = $4,888,214

Year 14, $4,888,214 x 1.06 - $80,000 = $5,101,507

Year 15, $5,101,507 x 1.06 - $80,000 = $5,327,597

Year 16, $5,327,597 x 1.06 - $80,000 = $5,567,253

Year 17, $5,567,253 x 1.06 - $80,000 = $5,821,288

Year 18, $5,821,288 x 1.06 - $80,000 = $6,090,565

Year 19, $6,090,565 x 1.06 - $80,000 = $6,375,999

Year 20, $6,375,999 x 1.06 - $80,000 = $6,678,559

Appendix 3 for Chapter 20

Year 0, Debbie and Doug have $1,800,000 in bonds, and $1,200,000 in mutual funds.

Every year, they sell $80,000 of their bonds to pay for living expenses. Their bonds return at 6% per year. Their mutual funds return at 8% per year.

Year 1, they sell $80,000 of bonds to pay for living expenses. Their bonds = $1,800,000 x 1.06 - $80,000 = $1,828,000.

Year 2, they sell $80,000 of bonds to pay for living expenses. Their bonds = $1,828,000 x 1.06 - $80,000 = $1,857,680.

Year 3, they sell $80,000 of bonds to pay for living expenses. Their bonds = $1,857,680 x 1.06 - $80,000 = $1,889,141.

Year 4, they sell $80,000 of bonds to pay for living expenses. Their bonds = $1,889,141 x 1.06 - $80,000 = $1,922,489.

Year 5, they sell $80,000 of bonds to pay for living expenses. Their bonds = $1,922,489 x 1.06 - $80,000 = $1,957,839.

Year 6, they sell $80,000 of bonds to pay for living expenses. Their bonds = $1,957,839 x 1.06 - $80,000 = $1,995,309.

Year 7, they sell $80,000 of bonds to pay for living

expenses. Their bonds = $1,995,309 x 1.06 - $80,000 = $2,035,028.

Year 8, they sell $80,000 of bonds to pay for living expenses. Their bonds = $2,035,028 x 1.06 - $80,000 = $2,077,130.

Year 9, they sell $80,000 of bonds to pay for living expenses. Their bonds = $2,077,130 x 1.06 - $80,000 = $2,121,758.

Year 10, they sell $80,000 of bonds to pay for living expenses. Their bonds = $2,121,758 x 1.06 - $80,000 = $2,169,063.

Year 11, they sell $80,000 of bonds to pay for living expenses. Their bonds = $2,169,063 x 1.06 - $80,000 = $2,219,207.

Year 12, they sell $80,000 of bonds to pay for living expenses. Their bonds = $2,219,207 x 1.06 - $80,000 = $2,272,359.

Year 13, they sell $80,000 of bonds to pay for living expenses. Their bonds = $2,272,359 x 1.06 - $80,000 = $2,328,701.

Year 14, they sell $80,000 of bonds to pay for living expenses. Their bonds = $2,328,701 x 1.06 - $80,000 = $2,388,423.

Year 15, they sell $80,000 of bonds to pay for living expenses. Their bonds = $2,388,423 x 1.06 - $80,000 = $2,451,728.

Year 16, they sell $80,000 of bonds to pay for living

expenses. Their bonds = $2,451,728 x 1.06 - $80,000 = $2,518,832.

Year 17, they sell $80,000 of bonds to pay for living expenses. Their bonds = $2518832 x 1.06 - $80,000 = $2,589,962.

Year 18, they sell $80,000 of bonds to pay for living expenses. Their bonds = $2589962 x 1.06 - $80,000 = $2,665,359.

Year 19, they sell $80,000 of bonds to pay for living expenses. Their bonds = $2665359 x 1.06 - $80,000 = $2,745,281.

Year 20, they sell $80,000 of bonds to pay for living expenses. Their bonds = $2745281 x 1.06 - $80,000 = $2,829,998.

References

Introduction

1. https://philosiblog.com/2012/03/26/freedom-lies-in-being-bold/#:~:text=%E2%80%93%20Robert%20Frost,lost%20the%20freedom%20to%20ride.

2. www.amazon.com/Million-Years-Real-Estate-Investing/dp/1716798450/ref=sr_1_1?dchild=1&keywords=david+Meng&qid=1605450772&sr=8-1.

3. Robert G. Hagstrom, The Warren Buffett Way, 3rd edition, 2014, p. 8.

4. www.serenitystocks.com/blog/was-benjamin-graham-rich-and-successful.

5. www.fool.com/investing/general/2016/02/15/our-5-favorite-warren-buffett-quotes.aspx.

6. www.catholiclane.com/church-has-a-duty-to-form-the-human-heart-in-god%E2%80%99s-truth.

7. www.reddit.com/r/btc/comments/6w4j5d/whenever_you_find_yourself_on_the_side_of_the.

8. www.goodreads.com/author/quotes/256172.Robert_H_Schuller.

9. www.brainyquote.com/quotes/dale_carnegie_132157.

1. Real-Life Examples of Planting Money Trees

1. www.fool.com/investing/general/2016/02/15/our-5-favorite-warren-buffett-quotes.aspx.

2. www.yahoo.com/now/advice-mark-cuban-warren-buffett-130047649.html.

3. www.pinterest.com/sandra8818/warren-buffet.

2. Conventional Wisdom Kills Financial Freedom

1. www.bls.gov/opub/mlr/2018/article/great-recession-great-recovery.htm#:~:text=In%20a%202%2Dyear%20span,million%2C%20or%20almost%206%20percent.

2. https://money.usnews.com/money/retirement/social-security/articles/2018-06-18/what-every-30-year-old-should-know-about-social-security.

3. www.caterergoodman.com/money-is-like-soap-the-more-you-handle-it-the-less-you-will-have-2/.

3. The Early Bird Gets the Worm

1. www.awakenthegreatnesswithin.com/35-inspirational-dave-ramsey-quotes-on-success.

5. Career Choice toward Wealth

1. www.forbes.com/profile/jim-simons/#1e58670b3b6a.

6. The Joy of Home Ownership

1. www.brainyquote.com/quotes/andre_rieu_476988.
2. www.businessblogshub.com/2012/07/will-smiths-greatest-quotes.

7. A Mortgage-Free Life Costs You Millions

1. www.goodreads.com/author/quotes/8276.Gaston_Bachelard.
2. www.brainyquote.com/quotes/thucydides_384481.
3. www.amazon.com/Million-Years-Real-Estate-Investing/dp/1716798450/ref=sr_1_40?dchild=1&keywords=real+estate+investing&qid=1609342224&sr=8-40.
4. https://acquirersmultiple.com/2017/06/how-to-invest-like-sir-john-templeton-in-2017.

9. Positive Carry

1. www.amazon.com/Million-Years-Real-Estate-Investing/dp/1716798450/ref=sr_1_40?dchild=1&keywords=real+estate+investing&qid=1609342224&sr=8-40.
2. www.pinterest.es/pin/571253533956200522.

10. My Crystal Ball Is in the Repair Shop

1. www.inspiringquotes.us/author/5328-theodore-roosevelt/page:2.
2. www.azquotes.com/quote/856550.
3. www.yahoo.com/news/weather/lies-damned-lies-corporate-earnings-194416701.html.
4. www.merrilledge.com/article/focus-on-time-in-market-not-market-timing.
5. www.ruleoneinvesting.com/blog/how-to-invest/warren-buffett-quotes-on-investing-success.
6. https://finance.yahoo.com/news/warren-buffett-dont-worry-economic-214342834.html.

11. Do You Have Cash Flow or Alligators?

1. www.inspiringquotes.us/author/2422-robert-kiyosaki/about-choices
2. www.businessworld.in/quotes/Suze-Orman-143.
3. www.amazon.com/Million-Years-Real-Estate-Investing/dp/1716798450/ref=sr_1_1?dchild=1&keywords=david+meng&qid=1608740889&sr=8-1.

12. Retire in Your 40s?

1. www.goodreads.com/quotes/8207347-stay-in-your-bed-as-long-as-you-want-your.

13. It's Not the Strongest, Nor the Fastest, But the Most Persistent, Who Succeed

1. www.passiton.com/inspirational-quotes/7477-ambition-is-the-path-to-success-persistence-is..

2. www.cnbc.com/2020/09/10/how-to-retire-early-using-real-estate-investing-and-rentals.html#:~:text=This%20couple%20retired%20at%2029%20on%20an%20%2488%2C000%20combined%20salary&text=Joe%2C%20now%2035%2C%20and%20Ali,around%2080%25%20of%20their%20income.

3. www.brainyquote.com/authors/calvin-coolidge-quotes.

4. www.advisorperspectives.com/commentaries/2019/06/13/this-time-its-different.

14. The Return Is the King

1. https://fm.cnbc.com/applications/cnbc.com/resources/files/2020/02/22/2019ltr.pdf

2. www.amazon.com/Million-Years-Real-Estate-Investing/dp/1716798450/ref=sr_1_1?dchild=1&keywords=david+meng&qid=1609441756&sr=8-1.

3. https://financialmentor.com/investment-advice/investment-mistakes/18076.

15. These Mutual Funds All Look Similar

1. Berkshire Hathaway Annual Reports 2019 as well as previous years.

2. www.marketwatch.com/story/hedge-funds-now-are-delivering-as-promised-but-the-winners-are-tough-to-find-2020-04-29.

3. www.cnbc.com/2019/03/15/active-fund-managers-trail-the-sp-500-for-the-ninth-year-in-a-row-in-triumph-for-indexing.html.

4. www.creditdonkey.com/average-mutual-fund-return.html.

5. www.aei.org/publication/more-evidence-that-its-very-hard-to-beat-the-market-over-time-95-of-financial-professionals-cant-do-it.

6. www.creditdonkey.com/average-mutual-fund-return.html.

7. www.mrgreatmotivation.com/2018/06/in-any-given-moment-we-have-two-options.html.

16. It's Just 1%. What's the Big Deal?

1. www.thebalance.com/mutual-fund-fees-1289688.

2. www.thebalance.com/what-is-the-average-mutual-fund-return-4773782#:~:text=If%20you're%20looking%20into,over%20the%20past%2015%20year.

3. www.nerdwallet.com/blog/investing/millennial-retirement-fees-one-percent-half-million-savings-impact/.

4. www.marketwatch.com/story/20-words-you-need-to-know-to-avoid-getting-fleeced-by-wall-street-2015-11-20.

17. Work Harder and Lose Money?
1. www.quora.com/How-much-does-the-average-person-make-in-the-stock-market.
2. www.tradeciety.com/24-statistics-why-most-traders-lose-money/.
3. www.forbes.com/sites/nealegodfrey/2017/07/16/day-trading-smart-or-stupid/#5642a3d41007.
4. https://medium.com/clays-thoughts/some-thoughts-on-risk-38548bb646ea.
5. Benjamin Graham. The Intelligent Investor.
6. www.cnbc.com/2017/05/01/7-insights-from-legendary-investor-warren-buffett.html.
7. www.rga-advisors.com/blog/why-average-investors-earn-below-average-market-returns.

18. This Sounds Too Easy to Be True
1. review42.com/what-percentage-of-startups-fail/#:~:text=An%20estimated%2090%25%20of%20new%20startups%20fail.&text=Around%2020%25.,to%20the%2015%2Dyear%20mark.
2. www.marketwatch.com/story/donald-trump-could-have-been-five-times-richer-2017-04-06.
3. www.berkshirehathaway.com/letters/2019ltr.pdf.
4. www.amazon.com/Million-Years-Real-Estate-Investing/dp/1716798450/ref=sr_1_1?dchild=1&keywords=david+meng&qid=1609171758&sr=8-1.
5. www.quora.com/Margaret-Bonnano-said-Being-rich-is-having-money-being-wealthy-is-having-time-What-do-you-think-of-this-quote.

21. The Eagle's Two Wings: Courage and Caution
1. www.brainyquote.com/quotes/baltasar_gracian_379621.
2. www.mavenadviser.com/blogcontent/investmentquotes.
3. www.brainyquote.com/quotes/maya_angelou_120859.
4. www.goodreads.com/author/quotes/2936846.Tacitus.

22. No Pain, Much Gain
1. www.goodreads.com/quotes/1388-a-ship-is-safe-in-harbor-but-that-s-not-what.
2.www.ameliaearhart.com/quotes/#:~:text=%E2%80%9CCourage%20is%20the%20price%20that,no%20release%20from%20little%20things.%E2%80%9D.

Disclaimer

This book serves as a helpful tool on investing. However, laws and situations differ from place to place. The reader should seek the services of legal, accounting and financial professionals, as such services are not provided by this book. Investing provides fruitful opportunities. However, investing also has the possibility to lose money, and events such as economic changes and local markets are not the responsibility of this author. While the author and publisher have used their best efforts to prepare this book, they make no warranties regarding the accuracy or completeness of the contents of this book. The author and publisher bear no liability, and the reader is responsible for his or her own investing loses and gains.

Also by David S. J. Meng

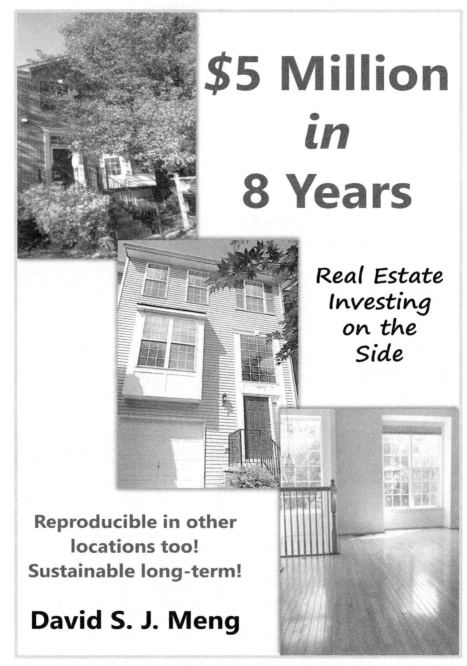

$5 Million *in* 8 Years

Real Estate Investing on the Side

Reproducible in other locations too! Sustainable long-term!

David S. J. Meng

Printed in Great Britain
by Amazon